Echoes From The Rocks

A collection of prose and poetry
written and edited by members of
The Knibs Writers Group, Killorglin

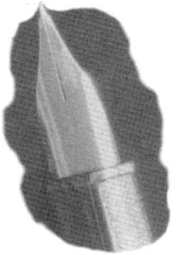

Published by Knibs

© Echoes From The Reeks

A collection of prose and poetry
written and edited by members of
The Knibs Writers Group, Killorglin,
is published by Knibs

July 2008

All rights reserved

All the contents of this anthology are copyright ©
to the contributing authors or their estates

ISBN 978-0-9559696-0-7

Cover photo, 'The Reeks' and the 'Knibs' logo appear courtesy of Val Lerigo-Jones
Cover & internal design by Mick Jones
Printed by The Killarney Advertiser

ACKNOWLEDGMENTS

Knibs are grateful to all those who have helped and encouraged us in the production of this book. We would particularly like to thank our sponsors below. Their generosity is greatly appreciated. We would also like to underline that we are not the only community group to benefit from the kindness of those listed; so we do hope our readers will in turn support those who have supported us.

Astellas Ireland Co Ltd, Killorglin

Bank Of Ireland, Market St, Killorglin

AIB, Iveragh Road, Killorglin

Captain Morgan Pubs Incorporated

Céad Míle Foto, Glounaguillagh, Killorglin

Dev's In The Square, Killorglin

FEXCO - (the global payments group) Iveragh Road, Killorglin

Killorglin Credit Union, Killorglin

Killorglin Furniture & Carpet Centre, Laharn, Killorglin

Mulvihills Pharmacy Ltd, Upper Bridge Street, Killorglin

Piano Express   (entertainments)   Caragh Lake, Killorglin

ACKNOWLEDGMENTS

In addition to sponsorship, we have received both direct and indirect support from a host of different individuals and organisations. Below are listed those key people. If we have accidentally omitted anyone from this list, please forgive us and be assured that your support is appreciated.

  Kerry County Council

Eibhlín, Margaret and Hazel, at Killorglin Library

Edso Crowley

Declan Mangan

Jerry Clifford

Eric Champ of Champ's EuroSpar

The Killarney Advertiser

'Echoes From The Reeks' is dedicated to the memory of
Carol Clifford
(1944-2006)

Carol was Chairperson of Knibs at the time of her sudden passing, just before Christmas 2006. She was the driving force behind the Knibs writers group in Killorglin. It's hard to believe that she left us so suddenly.

She worked as teacher and mentor to countless students, (many of them from overseas) studying English as a foreign language, and also discovering the culture and delights of Ireland under her guidance.

No task was too difficult for Carol. When Knibs published 'Ripples from the Laune', it was she who was at the heart of it. Soon afterwards, she had another venture in mind, a book of ghost stories. Accordingly, we have included a ghost story section in this collection.

Carol was a highly intelligent woman, with an intense love of Greece and the Greek language, and at the same time a simple person who loved the craic which we like to think of as a vital part of our Knibs meetings. She was possessed of a natural friendliness and an easy wit, which endeared her to all of us, and indeed to all who met her.

'Say not in grief that she is not here, but in thankfulness that she was.'

Contents

Carol Clifford	*Take Care*	9
Kate Ahern	*Ma, Da and The Lads*	10
Hazel Endean	*Words*	14
Team Knibs	*A Treat For Lunch*	15
Jo Scanlon	*Waiting For Jonno*	16
Mary Foley Taylor	*The Castle That Refused To Die*	18
T William Powell	*Ode To The Mini-skirt*	22
Mary Collins	*Scene Through A Window*	23
Mick Jones	*Paddy's Day 2007*	24
Hazel Endean	*Daylight Robbery*	30
Jo Scanlon	*Some Handy Irish*	31
Jack O'Dwyer	*Funerals*	32
Carol Clifford	*So Laugh With Me Now*	33
Jo Scanlon	*Life-cycle Of An Amoeba...*	34
Hazel Endean	*Dementia*	35
Mick Jones	*The White Strand*	36
T William Powell	*Home Thoughts From Abroad*	38
Kate Ahern	*Those Dancing Years*	40
Mary Collins	*The Lurcher and the Garden Party*	42
Hazel Endean	*Sam*	43
Carol Clifford	*A Star*	44
Carol Clifford	*How Then Reversed*	45
T William Powell	*Billy's List*	46
HazelEndean	*The Good Old Days*	48

Contents

Carol Clifford	*Seeds And Seasons*	51
Jo Scanlon	*Digressions*	52
Mary Collins	*The New Doctor*	55
T William Powell	*The Flight Of The Water Chestnuts*	56
Hazel Endean	*Watercolour Magic*	58
Carol Clifford	*Soul Search*	59
Kate Ahern	*Confirmation / The Dress Of Gold*	60
Mary Collins	*The Pound Note*	63
Carol Clifford	*Listen*	64
Hazel Endean	*Roses*	66
Hazel Endean	*Poor Myrtle*	67
Jack O'Dwyer	*Ghost Stories*	69
Mick Jones	*A Normal Tuesday Evening*	70
T William Powell	*Last Night*	72
Mick Jones	*House Down The Road From Us*	75
Jo Scanlon	*Through The Keyhole*	76
Mary Collins	*Ghosts At Home*	78
Mick Jones	*Restless In The Reeks*	80
Team Knibs	*Life At Ninety-Nine*	88
Kate Ahern	*Caragh Lake*	89
T William Powell	*The Crime Of Letdown and Punishment*	90
Hazel Endean	*Shelters*	94
Carol Clifford	*Which Piece is Home*	95
Jo Scanlon	*Killorglin Then And Now*	96

Preface

Writers groups proliferate across Ireland, and of course they are as varied as the individuals who gather to participate in their delights. Knibs does have its own claims to uniqueness, though of course, ironically, there's nothing particularly unique about that particular fact. The Knibs group though has the advantage of a home town that must be in the Premiere League of friendliness, which might explain the motley collection of locals and blow-ins that make up the membership.

As members we are certainly diverse enough, but we probably do have at least three qualities in common. First, our shared delight in writing; second, our sense of privilege at living in the beautiful County Kerry; and thirdly, the simple fact that if talking were an Olympic sport, Knibs could easily be the team to 'talk for Ireland'.

So, switch off the telly, the radio and the computer, find a quiet corner, a garden bench, a remote beach; just somewhere, anywhere to take a bit of time for yourself and... enjoy the mix.

Carol Clifford

Take Care

Writing is joy
Balanced with guilt, its foil
A blank page, no child's toy
Not to be used uncarefully
To slight, wound, or sting
No gossip columnist's raison d'etre
No old man's last fling

Take care
For the pen will last
Far longer than you dream
It will shatter like a glass
The secrets within,
Its power to harm testified by the past
Authors to whom reputations
Were only as grass

Kate Ahern

Ma, Da And The Lads

My Ma was a small dainty woman. She always wore her hair in a bun or chignon. An old woman told us that Ma and Dada were the prettiest couple she ever saw going into Church on their wedding day. Da had a fine head of coal black hair, he was a medium sized man with a black moustache. There were nine children in our family; seven boys in a row. The youngest boy was nicknamed Doc at home, as the seventh son was supposed to have a cure. Then we two girls arrived. They loved us all, but I am sure we girls were their pride and joy.

We were all born at home with the help of the local kind and gracious midwife. We were all breastfed, there were two or three or more years between each of us. Money was very scarce in the early days of the twentieth century, but we were always well fed. Ma kept a flock of hens, ducks and geese. How I loved the rich flavour of the big blue duck eggs we used to have for breakfast every morning before going to school.

We lived on a small farm of thirty acres, given to us by the Land Commission. Dad set potatoes, cabbages, and oats, and we had our own bog where we cut turf every year. Ma baked the bread in the oven on the open fire, not so easy if the turf was damp after a wet summer. She always remembered our birthdays, and would make an apple pie and a round fruit cake for the occasion. She always made us feel special and tried very hard to have us spick and span for Sunday Mass and school or for any big, important occasion. She loved nice things. Snow-white half curtains always hung in the windows. Her secret was to use Reckitts Blue in the rinsing water. It was years before she could afford to buy the lovely tea set of blue and white bone china, which she carefully kept for the Stations when Mass was said in our house every four years. The Parish Priest would have breakfast in the room made into a parlour for the day. Ma would clean the house from top to bottom; what painting and scrubbing went on, and white washing outside too. I will never forget during the Second World war when paint was very scarce, and the young curate took a cup off our dresser for the salt for the Holy water and as the paint had not dried properly, he was left with some brown stain on his hand. Ma was embarrassed that morning but sure the paint did not dry that time for weeks as there was some ingredient missing from it. She hand sewed our school-pinafores which had two box pleats front and back with big hems, so that they could be let down as we grew. She would add a contrasting piece of material to our dresses as we grew taller.

The lads, my brothers, had broken her Singer sewing machine before I was born. We liked to swing on the wheel of the foot part which we used as a side table and which lasted for years. You daren't have your skirts above the knees in those days, your hair had to be neat and tidy. My sister and I always wore our black hair in plaits. Poor Ma had a busy time in the mornings plaiting our hair and ironing the ribbons. People always thought we were twins we looked so alike. Ma would read us stories at bedtime The one which we liked best was about Colette and Jean Valjean; we used to call him Jean Vaseline. He was so kind to Colette and brought her a big doll and clothes. It was years before I discovered that the story was from 'Les Miserables'. Ma would make the story nicer to suit us, as children.

We would buy The Irish Press each day and it would be read from cover to cover by all the family. As children, we enjoyed being members of 'Captain Mac's' club. When you joined, you got a certificate and brass badge bearing a map of Ireland. As the second world war raged through Europe, we kept a close eye on all the events. It was discussed around our fire in detail every night, we did not have a radio, or wireless as they were called then. On Sundays after Mass, Ma would buy groceries and sweets for us, in the small sweet shop in the village. The lady there and Ma had very different opinions on World War II; she thought Hitler would win the war, and even called her pet dog Rommel. Ma was right of course. Eamon De Valera was her hero. He would know what to do. "What a great man he was," she always said, "that we in Ireland stayed a neutral country during those difficult times." She used to give 2/- to Dev's party, Fianna Fail, every year. She needed it more herself sometimes, but people had very strong political beliefs in those days.

Sunday was Ma's Big Day when she dressed up in her lovely beige coat and a tan fur with a tiny fox head tied around her neck. A black toque hat on her head, she wore beige stockings and black court shoes. She did look elegant as she walked down the rough boreen and stony road to Mass. The toque hat was a gift from Vera Myles, whose father was both magistrate and doctor for Dingle. Ma did housework for Miss Myles in Dingle; in return, she visited us regularly over many years, but moved to Dublin when her father died.

Ma was a dab hand at the flowers; pansies of purple velvet with little yellow eyes grew in abundance in the garden and appeared every year. Big tall clumps of creamy lilies came into flower each June. Every three years she would divide the lilies and give them to friends or exchange for another plant; she would stake the red and white dahlias from the wind. It was the pink honeycomb ones I loved best. We would bring bunches of dahlias for the altar in the church. Ma loved that. It brought a blessing to us all she said. She trained the two hawthorn trees and shaped each of them like an umbrella. Under one, which overhung like a roof, was an old seat. We had pretend tea parties with the small coffee set Ma got very cheap at Hilliards sale in Killarney. The enjoyment we got from those Sunday evenings, and Ma put real tea in the teapot, and with some Marietta biscuits we would feel very grand and grown-up.

We always called my seven brothers, 'the lads'. They and Dada would help set oats, potatoes or cabbages which were always set in rotation. Crops were never set in the same place more than three years in a row. Then you might set hayseed, a good mixture of clover and fescue which gave sweet hay which the cows loved to eat. As well as the usual turf cutting, the lads also gathered big stones and put them in a low, long rick at the side of the road. These stones were then sold to the County Council. A big smoky crusher would arrive to break the stones down into smaller ones. This was a slow, noisy job which could take a week or more.

Our Da died a young man of pneumonia. In those days, we had no radio, but my father read a lot of books and exchanged them with friends and neighbours. He read by the light of an oil lamp hung on the wall which was our only means of lighting; apart of course from the candles which Ma was always so careful of, as net curtains would catch fire in seconds.

We sang around the fire in the evenings. Some of the lads had good voices. Kelly, the Boy from Killian, and The Irish Rover were great favourites. Ma would tell us stories from Uncle Tom's Cabin, but Topsy was my own favourite.

For nine or ten months a year, my two older brothers went to work with two neighbouring farmers in Ballyhar. Another brother was a baker at the village bakery, so he had to rise about 6.00am to go to work every morning. Ma would wash his aprons on the scrubbing board with lots of 'Sunlight' soap and hot water.

In later years, as jobs were so scarce locally four of my brothers joined the Irish Army and three of them joined the R.A.F. They also played Gaelic football with Listry and Jim went on to win an All Ireland with Cork County in 1945. John also played for Cork. They won the National League and travelled to America, a big occasion in those days. John with two other Kerrymen, Captain Ned Roche from Knocknagoshel, and Tom Moriarty from Dingle, were invited back to play for Kerry and helped the Kingdom win two All Ireland Finals in 1953 and 1955.

Football was always the main topic of conversation when the lads were at home. They were great sportsmen, not only playing GA, but also playing basketball and running cross country. Patrick, Paddy as he is known in Cork, (still alive at 93) played with the Dick Fitzgerald's, now Dr Crokes. Three of 'the lads', Jim, John and Patrick played and won three Cork County championships with Collin's Barracks, the army team in Cork.

Sadly, Ma never learnt to cycle a bike, something that might have allowed her more freedom. Her only transport was donkey and cart. She never had much money, but she had great courage and faith. Her sons played in Croke Park, but she was never there. She did see them play those games at the Fitzgerald Stadium in Killarney; and she was so proud. It's with great fondness I remember the simple innocent days of my childhood.

Life then was very difficult and harsh for women. There was a lot of loneliness as families emigrated to find work. We all left home, so Ma was all alone, except at holiday time, Christmas and Puck Fair. I am sure Ma and Dada and my departed brothers and sister are up in heaven praying for us and hoping we will join them some day.

Hazel Endean

Words

kindness, soothing sorrow;
heartache healed.

anger, spitting sarcasm;
expletives exploding.

love, penning poetry;
creating cliches.

print, inspiring images;
reflections roused.

secrets, whispering words;
intimate.

Isolated.

Team Knibs

A Treat For Lunch

It wasn't a promising start to the day, not with rain coming in through the back door, and the dead bird in the kitchen.

"Ah well, not to worry," thought Agnes as she went back to find her galoshes and boots, "at least I don't have to find something for lunch now." She opened the oven door and placed the dead bird inside it

Agnes obviously wasn't a good housekeeper. She would leave one task unfinished to commence another. She had planned to get some fish for dinner, but decided instead to take what came her way and cook this bird without giving a thought to the effects it might have on its consumers.

Remembering the problem with the rain, she went next door to ask Mary for the carpenter's phone number, but Mary was in tears, "The canary's gone!" she wept helplessly.

Agnes put her arm round Mary and said, a tad cheerfully considering her long time friend and neighbour was in tears, "Don't worry Mary, come round for dinner with me, I've got a lovely surprise already cooking." Mary sank to the floor, subsumed by her friend's bizarre reactions, and cried all the more.

"Agnes" she said, "I cannot eat a dinner until my canary is found. Will you come with me and look for him please." "Right," said Agnes, "we'll start the search in my kitchen." Having arrived in Agnes' house Mary screamed, "These are my canary's feathers on your table!" and she collapsed on the floor.

"Oh dear!" sighed Agnes, "now I have two bodies to deal with."

One of the regular exercises at Knibs sessions, is to write an opening sentence, then pass it on round the circle for each member present to add a following sentence or two. The above is an example of such an exercise. The contributors were Mick, Tim and Jo.

Jo Scanlon

Waiting For Jonno

SCENE   The Square, Killorglin

Sheila: You didn't go home yet, Mary.

Mary: No, I'm waiting here for the last half-hour for that husband of mine.

Sheila: Don't worry Mary, he probably met some fellow who kept him talking.

Mary: Now Sheila. You know, and I know, and indeed the whole parish knows that Jonno is too fond of the drink.

Sheila: Ah well, now he's a good sort - nice and sociable.

Mary: Yes, when he is sober. But I'm telling you, Jonno drinks like a fish. It would be all right if he drank what the fish drinks.

Sheila: Why don't you go into the pub and tell him that you want to go home?

Mary: Well! I won't do what I did the Puck before last.

Sheila: And what was that Mary?

Mary: He went to the fair the first day and never came home that night. The second evening came and no sign of him. So I walked into town. I knew very well where I would find him. In I went to the pub and there he was sitting with his cronies. And what do you think he said to me?

Sheila: I don't know. That he was sorry maybe?

Mary: Sorry, how are you! He stood up with a smile on his face,

	put out his hand and said, "Wish a welcome to Puck, Mary Sullivan."
Sheila:	Well I wouldn't doubt him. He always had the bit of humour. And I suppose there was a big crowd in there looking at you.
Mary:	Packed to the door, girl. And do you know, there were as many young girls there as men, all sitting up on their high stools with their glasses of beer or whatever and dressed in their shrunken little tops, just like the ads on television.
Sheila:	Sure Mary, Puck is the time of the year for diversion.
Mary:	Well if it is, Jonno has Puck every day. He has me heart broke. I walked out of the bar, hired a taxi home and told Jack the driver to charge it to Jonno, which he did.
Sheila:	You did the right thing Mary. My husband Jim now, he never goes near a pub, sits down at night reading the paper and watching telly and chatting away.
Mary:	Glory be to God, that would be worse. You'll never see Jonno under my feet around the house.
Sheila:	The bus is coming Mary. I'll have to run.
Mary:	Do you know Sheila, I think I'll go with you. I have my free pass. I'd be better off waiting at home than here on the side of the street.

Mary Foley-Taylor

The Castle That Refused To Die

As any visitor to Ireland will tell you, Ireland is a land of castles. Some are well preserved and through them you can experience what life must have been like for the people who lived during that period of time. Other castles are just lonely ruins, almost crying out for recognition; symbols of better days and much different times, such as Castleconway in Killorglin.

On the famous Ring of Kerry, if you travel westwards along the river Laune you will be surrounded by the beauty of the landscape; as the peaceful river winds its lazy way to the Atlantic through Castlemaine Harbour, the towering McGillycuddy Reeks keep a majestic watch over everything.

As you make your way through Killorglin, you may be reminded of Puck Fair. Puck Fair is an old festival held every year for three days in August. Its origin is lost in antiquity but there are a few theories. One says during a Viking raid, sometime between the ninth and eleventh centuries, a herd of wild goats disturbed in the mountains, ran into town, thereby alerting the inhabitants of the forthcoming danger. Other versions say the incident happened during Cromwell's times, which may be farfetched as the owner of the town at that time was reportedly one of Cromwell's soldiers. Another belief is the fair had its origin as a pagan fertility rite. In 1601 a British royal Charter was granted for the holding of the fair. Whatever its origin, Puck Fair is a celebration not to be missed.

During Puck Fair a wild goat from the nearby McGillycuddy mountain range is crowned King of the Fair for three days. It is a very festive time all round during which time it is estimated over 100,000 people visit Killorglin, many of whom are emigrants from the area, returning to meet with old friends. Killorglin has a normal population of 1,500 people.

However, one thing that has almost been lost in history is that Killorglin was a much sought-after territory during the reign of Queen Elizabeth I. Killorglin, which had belonged to the Earls of Desmond since the thirteenth century, was included in the territory confiscated during the Munster Plantation. Among the names included in Elizabeth's plantation were Denny, Crosbie, Herbert, Blennerhassett and Conway. Through his connection with Queen Elizabeth's secretary of state, Jenkin Conway was granted more than 1,300 acres, which included Killorglin and its surrounding territory. Jenkin Conway was required to live in the area, so in 1587 he built his castle on the ruins of the former Desmond Castle destroyed during the various wars. Originally built in 1214, this castle seems to have been burned and rebuilt again in 1594.

Jenkin Conway was succeeded by his son, also named Jenkin, about 1610. The estate then eventually passed to Conway Blennerhassett, whose son, also Conway, then had three sons and six daughters. The relevant section of their interesting family tree can be seen on p21.

All six of Conway Blennerhassett's daughters married well, but his two eldest sons died very young which meant that the third son, Harman Blennerhassett, unexpectedly inherited Castleconway. Harman Blennerhassett was a man described by an acquaintance as 'having every sense except common sense'. He was educated at Trinity College, Dublin, where he counted among his friends Robert Emmett as well as his brother Thomas Addis Emmett, who were also distantly related.

In 1790 Harman became a lawyer, although he had no need to ever practise law as he inherited Castleconway in 1792, leaving him worth almost £50,000, which was an enormous sum of money at that time. He was now one of the idle, very rich, gentry. In 1793 he joined the United Irishmen. He was also the last resident landlord of Castleconway.

One of Harman's sisters, Catherine, married Captain Robert Agnew, lieutenant-governor of the Isle of Man. In 1796, while a guest at the Agnew home, Harman was asked to chaperone Margaret Agnew, his niece, home from school. Although almost twenty years her senior, Harman married Margaret, in spite of very strong family objections. Such a marriage between uncle and niece was also illegal in Ireland. Being frowned upon by family and friends, the resulting alienation and Harman's reported involvement with the United Irishmen, no doubt influenced their decision to emigrate to America.

By 1800 the Blennerhassetts moved in to their paradise island on the Ohio River. It was a place of magnificence and culture, which attracted the attention of the then Vice-President of the U.S., Aaron Burr. Being such romantic dreamers, the Blennerhassetts were easily convinced by Burr to part with their money, to advance Burr's treacherous schemes, which included setting up his own government in what is now Texas.

Along with Burr, Blennerhassett was arrested for treason. Although later acquitted, Blennerhassett was now a broken man. His property had been destroyed during the time of his arrest. In ill health, Harman, along with his wife, returned to Europe. The Burr-Blennerhassett trial was conducted by the then first Supreme Court Judge of the U.S., John Marshall. This would account for an island off Marshall, North Carolina, also being called Blennerhassett Island - to commemorate Marshall's (and indeed America's) most famous court case.

Harman Blennerhassett spent his last years in poverty and died on the Island of Guernsey in the Channel Islands in 1831, where a branch of the Agnew family had lived for almost a century. Margaret Agnew Blennerhassett then returned to the U.S. to petition the U.S. Congress to compensate her for the damage done by the militia to Blennerhassett Island, but died before the courts could issue a decision. Her attorney was Robert Emmett, son of Thomas Addis Emmett. Thomas Addis Emmett had become the Attorney General of New York State. The Emmetts cared for Mrs. Blennerhassett at the end of her life, and Margaret Blennerhassett was buried in New York with her friend Mrs. Emmett, but has recently been re-interred in Blennerhassett Island. The paradise that was Blennerhassett Island is today restored to its former glory and is a National State Park of the U.S. At present, it is planning for the upcoming bicentennial celebrations.

Meanwhile, back in Killorglin, Castleconway was inhabited until 1844 and then once again returned to being a ruin. It had come in the way of modern progress, as well as being a reminder of the English rule in Ireland. Unsuccessful attempts were made to demolish what was left of the ruin. But it refused to die. It was reportedly once used as the Puck Fair stand. Today it is scarcely visible and inaccessible to the public as it is on private property and the town was built around it.

However, some of the neighbouring buildings are now disused, so perhaps it would be possible to once again honour Castleconway for some of its former glory. Perhaps it would be fitting to jointly celebrate the revival of Castleconway in Killorglin, County Kerry, Ireland along with Blennerhassett Island on the Ohio River, in West Virginia, U.S.A!

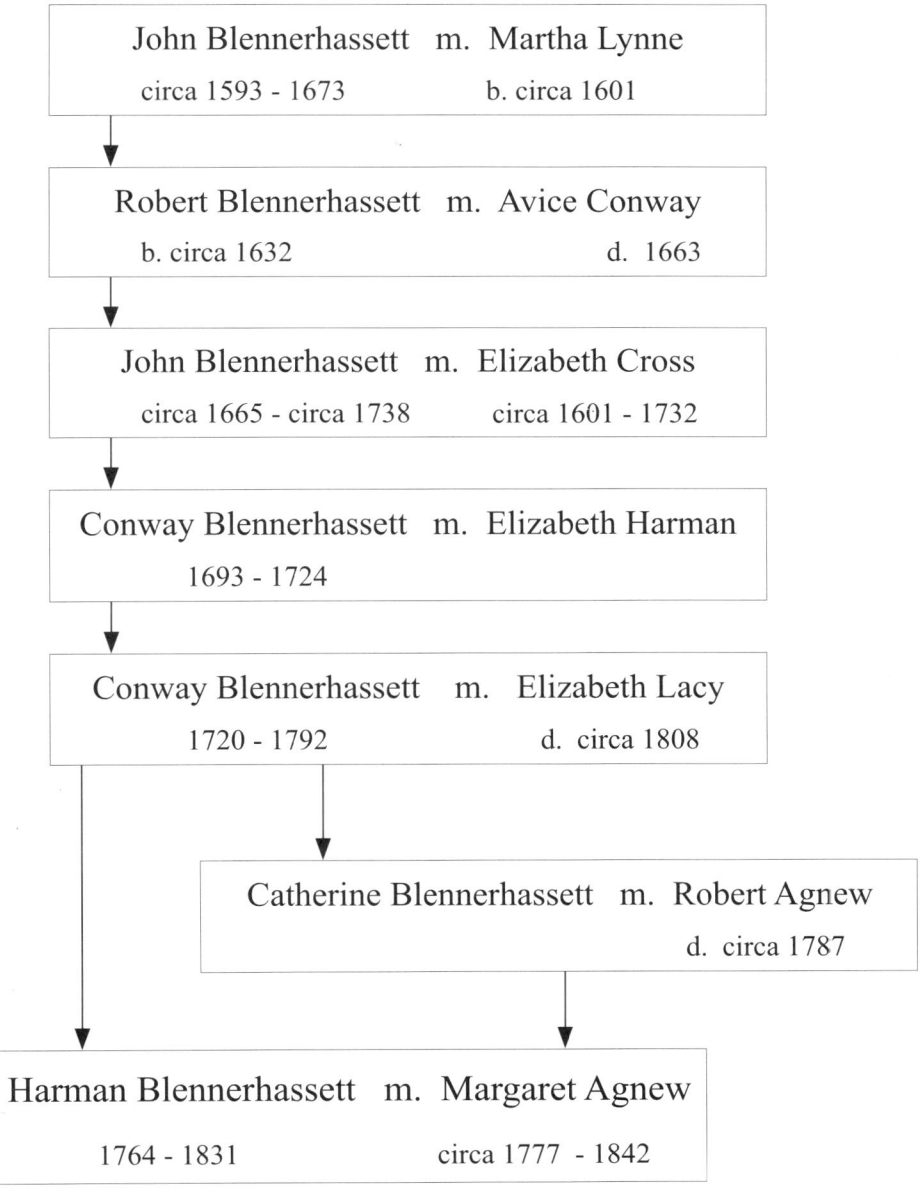

T William Powell

Ode To The Mini-skirt

We all need a raison d'etre, our very own reason to be
For the 1960s mini-skirt: to be at least four inches above the knee
Be you in Carnaby Street or Grafton Street, it really didn't matter
The mini-skirt had just arrived, decorum and deference to shatter

One piece of clothing, that's all it was, whyever such a fuss?
It made things so much livelier, sitting across from you on the bus
Especially if you hitched a bit, to get your ciggies out
Hosanna! Jaysus! Praise the Lord! One really had to shout

It's just a piece of apparel, its place in history made
Sweeping ball gowns and dungarees, leave them in the shade
What harm indeed to wink at you, to have a little flirt
To contemplate life's possibles, god bless your mini-skirt

I wonder what became of you, beyond our teenage bluster
Did you grace the shores of foreign lands, or stay home in a fluster?
Maybe you married, had ten kids, or tore through several glass ceilings
It's poignant to recall those days, of young unfettered feelings

But anyway, I hope you made it to the places that you sought
So many years ago that was, it's time I gave you some thought
It isn't Shakespeare, Keats, or Yeats, this quasi-poetic blurt
But I toast the memory of you now, and of your mini-skirt

Mary Collins

Scene Through A Window

Miss Penny lived in a big old house - the sole remaining part of the big estate which her family had owned. She was the last survivor and lived alone in this big ugly house, looked after by her old housekeeper.

Every afternoon she sat by the window in the top storey from 2.00pm and gazed out. The gardens, flower beds and lawns were now replaced by a housing estate. Her view instead was the backs of all these houses; what was she looking at? She had never met any of the people who lived in these houses and they, in their turn, wondered what she was looking at. Was she reliving the past when she was a young girl playing in the lovely gardens? Surprisingly, she was very much living in the present, fascinated by the lives of the people living in these houses. Aided by binoculars occasionally, she was charting their lives.

The house nearest her was occupied by a man and woman, presumably married, no children. Peace reigned until the 'husband' came home from work in the evenings; then the battle started or continued, voices were raised and sometimes blows exchanged until night fell and peace was restored for the time being.

This continued for several days until finally things escalated; they had moved out of doors and at this stage, physical violence was the order of the day. The husband appeared brandishing a hefty piece of wood with which he hit his wife. Miss Penny could hear the crack of the skull, the woman lay there lifeless and the husband disappeared. She heard a car start... he had gone. The woman lay immobilized. Miss Penny alerted the police, who came to investigate the scene.

As a result, Miss Penny was forced into the public eye and soon after left her old house. She moved into sheltered housing to resume a more normal way of life.

Mick Jones

Paddy's Day 2007

Say 'St Patrick's Day', and what do you think of?

Guinness, parades, flags, parties, the list could be a long one, could it not?

And then on the other hand, what things would you not associate with Paddy's Day? Obviously, a far longer list. For instance, Buddhism, dolphins, intergalactic travel, kiwi fruit or even... cricket? At this point, some readers may be leaping ahead, and some even in the right direction. Yes, it fills me with pride to share the fact that on Paddy's Day 2007, I was not in an Irish pub drinking Guinness, not in Ireland, nor even in Europe. No, I was watching a cricket match in Sabina Park, Kingston, Jamaica. Now are you with me? I am one of a select club who can say that when the Irish cricket team pulled off one of the all time greatest upsets in sporting history... I WAS THERE!

The game between Ireland and Pakistan was so much more uneven than the scrap between David and Goliath! In fact, it's hard to think of a parallel. Even small soccer teams who have embarrassed the great teams over history, usually have a long tradition of playing the game. A cricket team with a real Irish identity is, with some notable exceptions, a pretty modern affair. But, let me not digress into history and politics, you must be dying to know what happened on that extra-special 17th March.

For me, it started very badly indeed. Following the tie with Zimbabwe on the Thursday (15th), I celebrated with a meal at our hotel, but by the early hours of Friday, I was suffering possibly the worst stomach pains of my life. I wasn't just in agony, I was genuinely scared. I could hardly stand up, much less walk about! I was in a really bad way. However, after what seemed like a lifetime of searing pain, vomiting, and vain attempts at some respite in sleep, morning finally came around. The hotel nurse arranged for me to visit a local doctor, (no witch doctor jokes please) who was great. He assured me my pains were routine, (Yeah right! I thought) prescribed half a cupboard-full of pills, which cost about three and ninepence, and sent me on my way. Mercifully, the prescriptions seemed to work, and the pains had mostly subsided by Saturday morning; but I was still very uncomfortable, and nervous about being more than ten yards from the nearest toilet!

Still, I'd travelled to Jamaica to support the Irish cricket team; if I could stand up and walk, then I'd get to that game if it was the last thing I did. At the time it felt as though it might well be. But there we were, Val and I, in the George Headley stand... for the second time in three days. Somehow, I just had to get through the day. I could not, in my wildest dreams, have imagined what was about to happen.

The atmosphere was simply amazing. Three thousand or more Irish fans, flaunting every sort of symbol of Irishness you could imagine. There was almost no support for Pakistan, because to them, this was just a formality. Many Pakistan supporters only bought tickets for the second round! The Jamaicans on the other hand, had been genuinely impressed with both the performance, and the spirit of the Irish side playing against Zimbabwe; word had spread, and they turned out in good numbers. Also, they were just loving the idea that Pakistan could get knocked out of the tournament if there was a freak result. At 10.00am, nobody really anticipated that would happen, but the Jamaicans had decided they would get behind the Irish fans and their team anyway. So the three thousand Irish supporters had a few extra allies (a couple of thousand extra maybe) in the locals who chose not to be neutral for the day.

Pakistan batted first. I only discovered recently that the wicket was unusually 'green' for a Caribbean ground. Good news for the Irish bowlers; the right kind of surface for their kind of bowling. There were only seven runs on the board for Pakistan when Mohamed Haffeez edged a ball from Dave Langford-Smith to the wicket-keeper. The ground erupted! This was the perfect start. In general, it's quite normal for batting sides to lose an early wicket, but then recover and put a great score together, so although rejoicing was in order, no one was getting over-excited at this early stage of the day.

When the second wicket fell with only fifteen runs on the board, there was an even more deafening roar, and the excitement really started to build. Pakistan were 15 for two against Ireland! I pinched myself, remembered my gut problems and tried to forget it again. Then, as so often is the pattern, the Pakistanis started to rebuild; fifty runs on the board now, but no more success for Ireland. Then, to my utter amazement, with 56 runs on the board, the third Pakistani wicket fell. This was beginning to get very interesting indeed. At the time I didn't notice that my stomach pains had almost completely subsided, only later did I reflect on that. I was chatting to a Jamaican fan a few balls later when another roar went up. I'd missed the action! Me and my big mouth...

what had happened? When I found out, I was genuinely, and completely dumbstruck! The Pakistan captain, Inzamam-ul-Haq, had been caught with only one run to his name on the board. Incredible! So far Pakistan had scored only 58 runs for the loss of 4 wickets.

For those unfamiliar with cricket, that's a great bowling performance, and the type of score that makes a batting side nervous, and prone to more accidents! I struggled to make sense of what had just happened. It was now becoming difficult to come to terms with reality. For this particular supporter, that wicket was the pivotal moment of the match. Inzamam is one of the truly great batsmen. He is a destroyer of bowling sides. A stocky man, he is known to be hopeless at running between the wickets; he nevertheless regularly accumulates huge scores by repeatedly dispatching the ball to the boundary with the utmost ease. He is an iconic figure in Pakistan, and the loss of his wicket at this stage was, in my view, a body blow to his team. Incidentally, Andre Botha who took Inzamam's wicket, finished with figures of 8 overs (48 balls bowled), and took two wickets for a total of only 5 runs. That is an extraordinary personal performance in any form of cricket. Against Pakistan, it's a truly amazing achievement.

Before I moved to Kerry, I was a Worcestershire supporter. I've witnessed countless matches and clapped and cheered, politely of course, as is the English way. As each Pakistan wicket fell, the Irish fans grew in confidence and excitement, and I, like every single one of the three (or was it five?) thousand, was not just clapping, I was roaring!

A small Jamaican boy came up to me shyly, and asked if I had a spare Irish flag to wave. I most certainly did. I told his mum that he could have it, and keep it, as long as he waved it when we played against the West Indies a few days later. I got a huge beaming smile from her, she knew I was teasing.

So finally, the morning's cricket closed with Pakistan bowled out for 132. The Irish boys had bowled beautifully, fielded with both professionalism and commitment, and took their catches brilliantly. They hadn't fielded so well against Zimbabwe, and I heard a number of locals talking about how the Irish had raised their game for this big event. Those Jamaican boys know their cricket, they were absolutely right. So there we were: exhausted, elated and dying for the lunch-break to be over to find out if Ireland could match their fine performance in the field with the right level of determination in the batting department. At lunch break, I remembered my stomach problems again… I ate almost nothing, but kept myself well topped up with fluids.

There's no shortage of places to get refreshments at the beautifully refurbished Sabina Park, but as the Irish opening batsmen walked to their creases, the food counters and bars were almost deserted. It seemed that people were only hungry for cricket. By lunchtime on that historic Paddy's day, Ireland had already shaken the world-wide cricket establishment. Pakistan, dismissed today for a fragile total of only 132 runs, were not just a great team, they were one of the favourites for this particular World Cup. For an inexperienced team like Ireland, scoring even a modest 132 would not be easy against some of the world's top bowlers, but just about everyone in the ground was starting to believe that the impossible might just be in the process of being proved possible. Personally, I still didn't dare to think in those terms. I'm one of those supporters who really doesn't mind his side losing; as long as they are genuinely fighting, what I want to see is a tough battle and a close finish. At this stage, I thought the Pakistani bowlers would be just too angry to let a shock result occur. Anger sometimes helps sportsmen and women to focus… but not always.

You may remember that my day had started badly. The Irish batting innings did the same. Bizarrely, the first two wickets fell at the identical scores to Pakistan, one for 7, and then at two for 15 both Jeremy Bray and Eoin Morgan were back in the pavilion with their contribution to the match completed. Worrying! Enter wicketkeeper-batsman Niall O'Brian. The significant advantage that the Irish bowling performance created for the batsmen, was that they didn't need to score quickly, less than three runs per over is usually 'gettable' even by a side that's struggling. The key question was, could Ireland survive the 50 overs? If they could, they would almost certainly have accumulated enough runs to win. Niall O'Brian did not slam the Pakistani bowlers left right and centre, but crucially, he survived. That was really not easy. Those Pakistani bowlers were angry alright, but as it happened, maybe not entirely focussed. Now and then you sensed they were getting nervous too. When a batsman stays at the crease, confidence grows, and opportunities for boundaries start to present themselves. Niall's innings was a match winning performance; the top score amongst the Pakistani batters was 27. But against one of the top bowling sides in the world, Niall O'Brian scored 72 runs. a truly heroic contribution, and one which deservedly earned him man of the match. Sadly, he was out in the most embarrassing of ways. He had taken a liking to one of the spin bowlers and smashed a huge six deep into the crowd. Next ball, I was willing him to play safe, just settle for a single. Seven off the over would be plenty at this stage. No! Niall had glory, and an early finish in mind and went charging down the wicket swinging his bat for another maximum. He made no contact with the ball, and was out stumped! I was horrified; after such a fine innings, to get out in such a 'soft' manner was the last thing Ireland needed. Still, less than thirty runs to get, five wickets in hand, plenty of overs left, Niall's innings was good enough to be decisive; Ireland could and should get their shock result now. We just had to hope they didn't lose two quick wickets. When that sort of thing happens, nerves start to jangle, and things can go rapidly from bad to worse.

What happened next? You guessed it! Ireland lost two quick wickets. By this time I was in shreds. I was beginning to think I should have booked a private ambulance in case I needed hospitalisation. I wasn't worried about my tummy anymore, it was my heart I was concerned about. I have been lucky enough to enjoy rude health over the years, I've had no heart problems yet, (touch wood) but at that point in the match I was worried about my heart! I have never been to such an epic sporting event. To say the atmosphere was electric doesn't even begin to describe it, I'm going to have to cop out and say… you had to be there! When Ireland captain Trent Johnston came to the wicket, sixteen more runs were needed for Ireland to win with just three wickets left to fall. This was just too nerve-wracking. All the religious types were praying, all the heathens like me were trying to telegraph and telepathize positive support, but almost everyone (there were a handful of Pakistani supporters there after all) was roaring for Ireland. Every ball survived was another battle won. Every run brought that impossible outcome a step nearer and was greeted with wild adulation from a crowd more intoxicated with tension than alcohol. Which is saying something! The tension really was almost unbearable. Although Ireland seemed to be creeping across the line, you knew that one more wicket taken could still be enough to turn the tide for the Pakistan team.

Then, finally, with just one run needed, Trent Johnson 'opened his shoulders'. If you don't follow cricket you might be wondering what I'm talking about. It's a cricketing term for smashing a ball way out of the field for the maximum six runs. In this case, not just any six runs. This was six of the most historic runs, and one of the most historic strokes ever to be struck in cricket. Ireland had beaten Pakistan by three wickets. Euphoric chaos erupted all over the stadium. Irish and Jamaicans were set for a very special party. And if the 'planet earth authorities' were looking for two races to represent them in an inter-planetary partying contest, Irish and Jamaicans would almost certainly be on the shortlist. I was breathless. It seemed that during the day my stomach had recovered, the question for me now was, would my heart?

Well, I'm still alive to tell the tale, so clearly, I pulled through. The combination of medications, and drastically reduced food intake, seemed to have worked, and I slept through most of Sunday. Then the news of Bob Woolmer's (Pakistan coach) death broke. We were in a hotel just 100 yards or so from where it happened. It's hard to understand, how with today's incredibly sophisticated science, the police and medical investigators could get things so badly messed up. Poor Mrs Woolmer. I'm sure I'm not the only one who felt that she was the real victim. To lose a husband so well respected, tragic enough, but to have to deal with all those rumours and gossip amidst her grief? I sincerely hope she and her family find peace somehow.

By Monday I was well enough to get about again. I wore my Irish T-shirt with greater pride than ever. In Kingston, a white face in Irish cricket colours was a VIP. Wherever we went, the locals just wanted to wish us well... as long as we didn't do the same to them on Thursday. Then they would laugh and say, "...but dere's NOAAHH chance a dat mon!" They were right again, they do know their cricket after all!

I left Jamaica with an extra-ordinarily vivid memory of an epic sporting event. I hope so much that Ireland can build on their World Cup success. The road ahead for Irish cricket is not going to get any easier, I hope the media don't start falling into the old trap, churning out those journalistic clichés, waffling on about 'golden ages'. That brilliant performance in Jamaica against Pakistan could, ironically, be a millstone to future sides if too much expectation is burdened on them. In my humble opinion, what Irish cricket needs most is a load more supporters getting right behind them all the time, win or lose. C'mon Ireland, show those boys the fan loyalty they deserve. They really have earned it. If you've never been to a cricket match, maybe you should give it a go. You'll be lucky to see anything as exciting as the 2007 Paddy's Day match against Pakistan, but if you see the Ireland cricket team fight even half as hard as they did that day, you will not be disappointed.

Hazel Endean

Daylight Robbery

As you flit
from flower to flower,
sucking golden nectar on your tongue.
Little do you know it,
but soon your efforts will be wasted.
I feel a sense of guilt
before the job's begun.

Like a spaceman
I walk slowly
towards your throbbing hive,
hating to disturb you
in your warm cocoon.
All too soon,
like suicide bombers
you sting and die together
to protect your precious hoard.

Soon the hive is empty;
for those left behind,
a feeling of anger fills the scented air.
You have fought and lost
the battle, but beware,
any living thing within your reach
you will attack,
to the bitter end.

Spaceman's suit discarded,
hat and gloves lie on the floor.
Golden honey dripping,
from a tap.
Bees against windows and doors
to claim what is your right.

Too late,
you must start all over again
if you are to survive the winter.
"Will you think of us,
when you eat your toast and honey,
And remembering,
the damage you have done,
will it taste bitter-sweet?"

Jo Scanlon

Some Handy Irish

leamh (pr. lav)　　　　Bland, insipid or uninteresting. – *This dish is described as exotic. I don't agree, I've never tasted anything as leamh in my life*

meas (pr. mass)　　　　Respect or esteem.
I've no meas on that fellow as a leader. He has no ability.

cnáimseáil (pr. knawvshawl)　　Grumbling or nagging
Jack's wife is forever nagging. He says he would sometimes rather have a blow of her fist than all the cnáimseáiling.

gligín (pr. gligeen)　　　Silly brainless girl.
Take no notice of what that little gligín says. Her tongue will get her into trouble some day

taoscán (pr. tayskawn)　　Small quantity of liquid.
My tea is too hot. Put another taoscán of milk in it, please.

brus (pr. bruss)　　　　Small pieces or dust.
He jumped on top of the pile of turf and made brus of it.

leadránach (pr. ladránock)　　Longwinded.
Please come to the point and don't be so leadránach.

mí-ádh (pr. mee-awe)　　Bad luck or misfortune.
There is some mí-ádh on that team. They never seem to win a match.

clampar (pr. clowmpar)　　Dispute or wrangling. Mischief.
There will be clampar tonight when he accuses his cousin of theft.

Jack O'Dwyer

Funerals

Death is inevitable, but in olden times the funeral was more of a celebration of the life of the dead person. Hundreds of people turned up at the wake-house offering their sympathy to the bereaved. The men smoked clay pipes while they swapped stories about the departed; the women taking a pinch of snuff, prayed at the bedside. People stayed up all night at the home of the deceased until the time of the removal to the Church. Prayers were said throughout the night beside the remains and in other rooms.

Nowadays in some places, a funeral is private - confined to the family alone. There are no flowers allowed. Instead, money may be sent to various charities. The family home is closed to the public. The Funeral Home has almost taken over from the wake-house tradition. It is opened a few hours before the removal. In rural parts of Ireland families are represented by just a few members. The Rosary is said before the removal.

The vast majority of the dead are buried in a cemetery. In recent years the number of cremations has greatly increased. The ashes are sent to the family home, if requested, and placed in an urn on the mantlepiece. Some people express a wish to have their ashes buried in the garden, under a favourite rose bush, or perhaps at their favourite football ground. The saddest thing about cremation for those who had lived in the more rural parts of Ireland, is the absence of a funeral. This is simply due to the long distance to the nearest crematorium, which makes the usual celebrations impractical. However, in some cases, the urn containing the ashes may be buried later with all the funeral rites.

There was a time when unbaptised babies were buried in places outside the normal burial grounds. People could not bury their infants in sanctified grounds, so special plots had to be found. Such sites, which became known as 'killeens' were often in ancient, disused churches or graveyards, ruined abbeys or fairy forts. As late as the 1930's people might simply get a spade and shoe-box and go about a burial, often in the dead of night.

Coffins were often shouldered for miles to the graveyard, by teams of four men at a time. Motorised hearses didn't appear until the late 1940s.

Carol Clifford

So Laugh With Me Now

"Something funny" she said,
No can do, the muse fled
From my mind to another sphere,
Catch me if you can,
I'm just in your ear.

How did you get there?
And pray tell me why
I am floating in space
Whilst you, muse, are here?

I'm here in your ear
To drum up in your mind
Something funny
And to help you unwind
From your mortal coil
And to act as a foil
For the life left behind.

There is nothing so funny
As serious life
With it's sombre mistakes
And all of its strife

For we are but a flash in eternity's eye
A speck of dust that time will destroy
A moment in time which does not exist
So laugh with me now
While the Gods do the twist.

Jo Scanlon

The Lifecycle Of An Amoeba In A Sow's Ear

When the above was suggested as a subject for homework at one of our weekly meetings, I asked myself: "What is an amoeba?" I had heard the word, but no more. From the dictionary I learned the following: Amoeba: a microscopic aquatic one-celled organism constantly changing shape.

Aquatic! I assumed then that this organism needed water to survive. But how to get water in a sow's ear? Unless of course the sow dug its snout into the muck each day, thus ensuring a regular supply of liquid.

It was constantly changing shape; so I imagined it expanding and contracting in all directions. and perhaps sending out shoots, rather like arms and legs. As for its lifecycle, I had not the remotest idea. My scientific education has been sadly neglected, so I had to have recourse to a limerick.

There was a fat sow called Bathsheeba
Who bore in her ear an amoeba
It grew bigger each day
Winding round the sow's tail
Till she died of the strangest of fevers.

I hope that, having listened to this reading, you are all now far more enlightened on the very interesting subject of the amoeba. Thank you.

Hazel Endean

Dementia

It took ten steps across the room to reach your side; one for each year since we last met.

Then: we had talked and giggled like schoolgirls, deep into the night.

Now: I hardly recognise this matchstick doll as my sister and you don't know me at all. I sit and gently hold your hand; a white ice-cold skeleton. Placing the box on your lap, I feed you chocolates one by one. I talk, but you don't hear; you are only interested in the shiny box.

"Do you remember our games of table-tennis? How you nearly always beat me? And how we loved playing cricket on the beach!" Our eyes don't meet. More chocolates. "Remember those wonderful holidays in Cornwall?" But of course your real love was ballroom-dancing. I'll never forget the day you opened your wardrobe to show me at least two dozen dresses: like Aladdin's Cave, it shone with gold, and silver and coloured jewels. A far cry from the plain dark-blue shift you're wearing today; buttoned all the way, I notice, for convenience.

All too soon, it's time to go. I bend to kiss you goodbye when you whisper, "Are you taking me home?" Now it's my turn to be speechless. I want to cry out, "This is your home now!" but the words choke deep inside.

Through a haze of tears I take ten blind steps away from you and I can't look back.

Mick Jones

The White Strand

...following a visit to Rossbeigh

My feet flirt with the waters
At the edge of a washed white strand
I'm dizzy, like a child again
At the place where sea meets land

The quickness of my fingers
Leaves no mark upon the stone
Yet the strand sees deep into my soul
The beach knows I'm here alone

I hardly dare to breath in case
I tarnish this crystal world
I hold my breath till my dizziness
Drowns in the waters sparkling swirls

>Pebble, shale and shingle
>Shingle, shale and sand
>The craft of countless millennia captured
>Here in the palm of my hand

The day is like any other
The sea remains unconcerned
It has no need to worry or weep
Over lessons remaining unlearned

And when we tear our hair and sob
Over days that will not mend
The strand remains an innocent,
But true and constant friend

Yet of all those days that went before
And of all those days that still wait on
There are none will shed a single tear
When all of us are gone

       Pebble, shale and shingle
       Shingle, shale and sand
       The touch of countless millennia captured
       Here in the palm of my hand

Though who is so deaf they fail to hear
In this boisterous solitude
The days that danced to a sea breeze band
Setting soft and musical moods

The patience of each subtle wave
Smoothing away the years
The rhythm of this white noise land
Distraction for jaundiced ears

The tears of desperation spilt
By the lover, the rogue and the cheat
Dissolve in the watery sandy silt
And hope and forgiveness meet

       Pebble, shale and shingle
       Shingle, shale and sand
       The healing of countless millennia captured
       Here in the palm of my hand

T William Powell

Home Thoughts From Abroad

As of 24 hours ago, I have now been to The Great Blasket island. Not that that's going to change anything there, nor will it make any difference at all to the people who lived there, until fifty years ago. It's geographically the same place it ever was, on the global scheme of things one very small place, but I wonder how many places - anywhere, not just around Ireland and the UK - come close to having been such a distinct place, separated from other lumps of land where people live, which has been a complete living world for the people upon it. For 300 years or so.

Would I have even known where the Blasket islands were if someone had asked me, up to a year ago? Probably not. I didn't major in geography anyway, but it still seems faintly ridiculous to have lived not that far away on a neighbouring island and not even know of somewhere. To not have known that this was not just one little islet off Ireland, but a community within itself, where people were born and grew up, upon a habitat where fortitude and resilience would surely have been required to an extraordinary degree for anyone to survive, never mind live.

But folk **did** live on Great Blasket, and it's hard to learn much about the people that lived on the island without feeling that for many having to leave Blasket would have been utterly unwelcome. Over time, emigration - whether to Dunquin, Dingle or to America - gathered pace and the end of Great Blasket as a home became inevitable.

But it was home for quite a few people, a small number compared to the Irish population perhaps, but a very distinct community where support and working together was not merely a favour. It was the norm in lives lived together in a rugged, often relentlessly weather-ravished rock and hard place; a place I'd never been to till a day ago, which everybody had left before I was born. And yet a place I won't forget. It exudes history, and the belated Blasket Island Centre provides a form for that to continue.

It's one more place that never was nor ever will be home for me, but it has provided a sharp illustration of the importance of home, wherever that is, to most people. The Blaskets will probably never be home to anyone again, though it's already part-time home or work-place to a few people via its hostel and craft shop, and a place where the already-existing number of visitors is likely to continue to rise. It remains a small, but unique place in the increasingly global travel scene and one I'm glad to know.

So I have no place in the story of a community to which I do not belong, and even if I'd lived then I doubt I'd have survived long on Great Blasket; so where is home? Not the house I was born in and lived in for the years that are formative for other people - when you're stuck in Suffolk you're lucky to get out. Kent then? Well it was, until I sold up the home I had outside Canterbury and escaped the workers co-operative wholefood business I was a partner in, where, you seemed to work twice as long and hard as you did before we took over, for a smidgeon more money; or even longer, for even less. It made living on The Great Blasket seem like a doddle.

Across the water, living in the smallest home I've ever had with the MacGillycuddy Reeks outside and occasionally a cow or two wandering past the window, was a veritable blast. Now I've shifted along a bit, closer to Killarney.

I digress. No change there then. But I like being an outsider here in Kerry. Seems to me, home is wherever you want it to be, if you're able to make it happen. And anyway, I'm a writer, so home is where me and the muse get drawn to, or feel like pitching up. Thanks for listening, but I've got Crime & Punishment 2, a column for the New York Times, and countless reviews and critiques par excellence to work on, so gotta go.

Kate Ahern

Those Dancing Years

Every time I passed that roofless building in Killorglin, the old Oisin Cinema and Ballroom, (now the AIB bank) with its big window all boarded up, I remember the pleasure and fun we had. It brings back such happy memories of the enjoyment and romantic dreams it gave to so many people, young and old.

To me it was the Ballroom of Dreams, a place of wonder and excitement. I saw my first film there at eight years old. My sister and I walked four miles to the matinee, and I was afraid to go in at first, I was frightened of the dark.

In later years I would cycle there to see the big films: 'The Quiet Man', 'Gone with the Wind', 'The song of Bernadette', and 'Going My Way' which drew huge crowds; with big queues for tickets which was unusual in those days of the forties and fifties. There were three prices, four pence for the very hard backless seats in the front near the screen, ten pence for the middle rows, and one and three pence for the soft 'posh' seats in the back. To be asked to the pictures by the man of your dreams was a very rare treat in those days. You'd be walking on air, unless of course you were 'doing a strong line', in which case you would be asked in Confession whether you had the intention of marriage, or if you had any bad thoughts when company keeping.

Oh, the excitement of the Big Dances in that ballroom. I was only fifteen when I went to my first dance with my brothers and sister. It was Christmas time. I just loved dancing, and it felt like Heaven. The dances were usually held from 8.00p.m. to 2.00a.m. and at Christmas time from 9.00p.m. to 3.00am. Five shillings was the entrance price. Big bands like Mick Delahunty, Maurice Mulcahy and Jimmy Rohan of Tralee played there and most had a nine-piece band with a lead singer. They were dressed in black suits and bow ties and gleaming white shirts, very elegant!

If it was raining on the night of the dance I would wrap up my good dress and shoes carefully and put them in a brown string bag. Then I would cycle to the dance in Wellingtons and an old skirt and jumper, and of course a heavy coat and headscarf to keep out the rain. Everyone was greeted by the owner,

Duffy, with a smile and a "Hello" as you paid your money and wheeled your bicycle in the door into a side alley which was part of the premises. In later years there was a charge of sixpence for parking your bike. Then upstairs to the ladies room where there was a huge mirror. A quick change into the good dress and shoes, hair combed carefully, a dab of Evening in Paris perfume if you had it (two and sixpence for the tiny blue bottle), a little dab of Fond's lipstick and I couldn't wait to get downstairs. We were always in the hall on the dot of eight o'clock. There was a cloakroom in the ladies with a tiny window where you handed in your coat and the string bag. They charged sixpence and gave you a ticket. You took great care of it as you would have to wait for your coat if you lost it. Looking back, it was an innocent, magical place. That ballroom gave us our hopes and dreams. At that time there was mass emigration and it could be very lonely for those left at home. At Christmas and Puck Fair you met all your old school friends who were home on holidays from Dublin and England, and perhaps the odd one from America, always beautifully dressed and with gorgeous high-heeled shoes.

Fellas didn't worry too much about what they wore; just a plain grey or navy suit with a white or blue shirt, some of them would not even bother with a tie. You would get a whiff of a cow from a farmer's son when he was dancing with you; most of them would have milked eight or ten cows by hand before coming to the dance. The black-haired men would use Brylcreem to give their hair a shiny, sleek look. It was a great treat to be asked upstairs to the balcony to have a mineral with your dancing partner, and nearly always meant it was a certainty that he would see you outside after the dance for a bit of romance and a chat. Fellas usually saw their girlfriends 'inside' at the dances, as money was very scarce, and ten shillings for a couple was a lot.

Dancing in the fifties was frowned upon in our village, and when Duffy opened another ballroom four miles away which he called the 'Oscar', our fiery young curate pounded the pulpit and said it was an occasion of sin and we'd be damned if we went there. Sure enough it did pour rain on the opening night, but my friends and I had a great time. There were big crowds, but it never compared to the Oisin in atmosphere. The ladies room was icy cold in winter so we didn't spend too long making ourselves presentable there.

I have never forgotten those nights of magic and wonder, fun and companionship, in the great country ballrooms of the past.

Mary Collins

The Lurcher And The Garden Party

The country fair was run by the Lady of the Manor in the height of the summer season. It was really for the children, although the mothers were there in huge numbers, in their best garden party ensembles. The styles varied from anorak and green wellies to the gayest of summer's dresses.

All the fun of the Fair was there for the children - slides, lucky dips, races - both human and dogs, cake stall well attended, especially by my brood. You'd think they never had a decent meal in their lives. But the biggest attraction of the afternoon was the dog race. This was supposed to be for lurchers. But every pet dog of all breeds was lined up for the races. The lady of the manor had three lurchers: pure bred, who won every year. But this year there was one serious protagonist. And that was the reason I was there. My dog, whose name was Tristan was a very mixed breed but on the outside he looked the real thing. He was tall and leggy and black and I knew he was very fleet of foot.

So the time came for me and my dog. The starting point was a series of boxes with sliding lids. The course was 100 yards. The owners stood by the box which contained their dog with hands on lids. At the signal the lids were raised and the dogs released. What then happened I find hard to relate without crying. Tristan shot out - did a 180 degree turn and headed for the open country. Like his owner, he had no sense of direction!

I spent the remainder of the afternoon searching for him and after finally tracking him down, we slunk quietly home.

Hazel Endean

Sam

My heart bursts with love
for you,
Grandson:
whose gentleness
and understanding
belie eight short years.

Come,
Climb mountains with me:
fish rivers;
sail seas;
discover a world
beyond boundaries

No!
I must wait

For now,
you are content,
roller-blading on concrete.

Carol Clifford

A Star

Soft as the snowflake, sharp as a knife
Eyes of a street child, observing life
Smiles don't come easy on a barrio street
Hunger, death and corruption replace treats

Cheap is her life, her virginity too
Sold by her mother for pennies, too few
A star for a moment on a flickering screen
Soon succeeded by others, at five a has-been

She looks at the man who co-ordinated the show
The snowflake has melted, leaving nothing below
The sharpness has dulled; her eyes are now dead
As she stares at her future with not a word said

That child could be yours, well-dressed and fed
With the soft down of childhood, forever fled
Look in the eyes and catch the pain there
The unspoken words, spoken with care

The net is spread wide with evil supreme
For people are watching, minds dirty or clean
Money transacted, no cash changing hands
Children bought, sold and murdered
Is this really OUR land?

Carol Clifford

How Then Reversed

Parallel universe in a different time
Mirrored by ours in a swirling sphere
Little green men with dark open eyes
Little green children, what a surprise

They looked at us as the mirror cracked
We gaze back, stunned, felt attacked
Our instant response, flight or fight
Their's, curiosity at our might

They are from Mars, God of war
We are from Earth, Mother Goddess of all
How then reversed in this curious world?
How came we here, in time with their Sphere

T William Powell

Billy's List

I think it was finding the list in his pocket; that was when it finally hit me, like a southpaw to the face: Billy had gone. I mean, it's hardly that you don't know someone has left the land of the living when you've just been called to the morgue to identify his body, but cliches like 'sinking in' and the like...

Well anyway, there I stood in this place that exuded cold: literally, figuratively, cold, cold, cold... and out came Billy, rolled out on a metal tray and dead as Great Aunt Dodo up in Mississippi. The shock, if that's what it was, had hit me hours before when I'd first been told about what had happened, and that Billy was dead. Here, with what felt like this big black cloud from Appalachia hanging round me for hours, there was a strange and deathly numbness that seemed to surround me when out he came.

The times in my life when I'd longed for the situation where he couldn't say one goddamn word to me, and here it finally was.

"He's just been put in here till someone came to identify him, Ma'm", said the warder or whatever you call someone who pushes folk in and out of a human freezer. He just said that and waited, and I wondered what the hell he expected me to say.

"The cops said they'd just leave the stuff they found in his pockets till you'd seen him, M'am. Y'know, out of decency 'n' all, I guess."

"Oh" was all I could think of to reply with. I put my hand in one pocket and there was a dollar or two in there, a bus ticket, and then this scruffy bit of paper that I could see he'd written something on.

"Marlboro, eggs, rubbers, Buds, paper, Kath prez." His shopping list for the morning pop out to the shops.

I smiled at the usual things there, smiled at how he wrote a list out for stuff he always got anyway. But he was going to get something for me? The sonofabitch surprised me at times, but I'll never know what it was he planned to get for me that morning. I feel a tad guilty really as it wasn't exactly a bolt from the blue - another cliche, bear with me, you don't lose someone every day - that he'd gone, and I'd stopped thinking we were an ongoing thing a week or so back.

I think I was going to tell you that, next time I saw you y'know; when you got back with your Marlboros, your paper, your rubbers, your Buds.

But I hope you rest better in peace than you ever managed in life, Billy. I've no idea why my being there with your dead body brought back to me how we used to throw those Gilbert and Sullivan lines at each other. On our better days.

The unknown present from you that was to be heading my way, the unknown to you imminent ending of us by me. Well you're gone now my old crawfish, who never would be missed.

Who never would be missed.

'As some day it may happen that a victim must be found,
I've got a little list - I've got a little list
Of society offenders who might well be under ground
And who never would be missed - who never would be missed.'

The Mikado (1885) act 1, W.S. Gilbert (1836-1911)

Hazel Endean

The Good Old Days

"Could you drive me into town, Gran?" Or, "would you mind dropping me back to the beach, Gran?" Pleas from my grandchildren come thick and fast. I usually drop what I'm doing and oblige. I FEEL like saying, "WALK!"

We had no transport in our family, father never owned a car. Indeed, I never sat in one until my eleventh birthday when a cousin took me for a drive. I remember feeling sick all the way... I was not impressed!

Life centred around our Lancashire village where my parents owned the corner shop. A newsagent/post-office with a lending-library in one corner, it was the hub of village life in Rising Bridge. Mother sold drapery and hardware, cigarettes and 'twist' - black sticks of tobacco which she cut up and sold by the ounce to the old men of the village. They chewed it between broken teeth and spat out wherever they fancied. Father handed out pension money, postal orders etc. and gave advice on all the problems of his customers. He made time for people, gave his own money to help those in need and they loved him dearly.

Although we were surrounded by three cotton-mills, two chemical works and a meat-pie factory, we thought our place was beautiful; smokeless fuel and sand-blasting was in the far distant future. We played hopscotch, skipped on pavements, kicked balls and tin-cans on spare ground and skated on frozen millponds in winter.

The school playground was ideal for our first attempts on bikes and roller skates. Soon we felt free and confident enough to ride and skate down hills at breakneck speed. Miraculously, we survived without our parents knowing what we got up to.

Beyond the factories, wide open moorland beckoned. On school holidays we would leave home after breakfast, walk seven or eight miles to sit amongst the spongy heather and fish in a nearby stream; tadpoles and tiddlers tipped into jam-jars to take home. On this journey we passed the cotton-mill where my sister worked. As we went by the grubby windows she'd glance up, face red and glistening with sweat; a quick wave then back to work. The weaving-shed reverberated with the clanking of a hundred looms; unable to be heard above the noise, workers resorted to sign language to converse with each other. My heart went out to my sister, working in such conditions. I felt guilty that I was free to breathe fresh air and roam the moors, but happy too, knowing that a different future would be mine.

I felt privileged living in a shop, but I was never spoilt. At the age of twelve I had to take my turn delivering newspapers and magazines like my brothers and sisters had done before me. Father would call me at 6.30am every morning except Sundays. I sorted out papers, then set off with a bulging canvas bag over my shoulder. Streets would be filling up with men and women heading for the factories, clogs on cobblestones ringing in the still morning air. Our village reminded me of one big, happy family, all calling out to each other, everybody knowing everyone else.

Making my way up and down streets I found cottages and rows of back-to-back houses; I would continue up out of the village until I reached the edge of the moors. Often waist-deep in snow, face stinging against icy winds, I loved every minute of it; happy to do it, before school, then again in the evenings after school. Each season had its own special magic. Spring brought primroses struggling for survival in blackened hedges. Maypoles were prepared weeks before the 1st of May. A broom handle was decorated with ribbons and streamers and the hoop from a barrel was fastened to the top. A ribbon for each dancer was attached and finally, the May Queen was chosen.

Walking from house to house, we sang and danced and afterwards, back in our kitchen, the coins were shared out. We could afford a sherbet dab, some pink and white coconut chips and a few cherry lips. If the neighbours had been extra generous, we rushed to buy an iced heart shaped box which opened to reveal a tiny ring nestling inside. A delight never to be forgotten! Summers were hot; the drone of bees as we picked blackberries almost lulling us to sleep.

Christmas was special. Battling against blizzards, it was heaven to be invited into cosy homes, a steaming mug of Oxo ready and waiting on the table. While they scanned the racing pages, football results or horoscopes I soaked up the heat before venturing out again into the white world.

Every year without fail, a customer gave me a pink sugar pig, which I kept well into March before eating. The sparkle and roundness of it was lovely and I thought it a shame to spoil it. Occasionally I received a half crown - riches indeed! People were so kind, giving me small gifts from their simple, often deprived homes.

When I reached seventeen my paper-round drew to a close. I said goodbye to my friends and caught a bus daily to my office job in town; only six miles away but a different world completely. My Wellington boots and heavy coats made way for hush-puppies and two-piece suits. Gone were the chats with old people huddled by firesides. No more standing on hilltops, looking down on our village below; seeing in my minds eye, mother, in her floral apron, serving the customers. Change was inevitable and life would never be the same again.

As I come out of my reverie, my grandson calls "can you get the car out, Gran, and take me to play computer games at my friend's house?" Yes, I'm just about to say it: that four letter word that's fast going out of fashion. WALK!

Bring back the good old days!

Carol Clifford

Seeds And Seasons

Purple flower
Dripping rain
Bleeding stems
Heart in pain

Bright green leaves
Spring again
Sun-filled showers
Pains sweet ease

Summer day
Seared and shrivelled
Colour faded
Roots bewildered

Winter cold
Bare stem old
Wrinkled weathered
Seeds of gold

Gold and purple
Regal colours
Hope and calm
Peace discovered

Jo Scanlon

Digressions

<u>Ladies Football Club</u>   <u>Committee Meeting</u>

President: Welcome Ladies. This is a very important meeting, I hope everyone is present.

Joan: Well, Carmel is not here of course. She had twin girls this morning.

President: Oh, I never heard it! Boys or girls?

Joan: Two little girls. She has her hands full now with one boy and two girls.

Mary: I'd love to have twin girls to be dressing them up in style. How did the little boy take the news?

Joan: Oh, he wanted a brother, but when he saw them, he said it was all right, because they looked like boys anyway.

President: No football for Carmel for a long time. We must send her a card. Now we have a big agenda to-night. You all know of course, that our match against Killarney ladies will be here on Sunday, and we would like to entertain them as well afterwards.

Mary: No trouble at all. We'll all help.

President: I would like every club member to bake a cake or a tart. Will you all spread the news, and try not to get all tarts and no cake.

Mary: Oh girls, I'm no good at baking. I made a tart the other day and the juice all ran out of it and stuck to the pan!

Peg: Mary, if you sprinkled some flour on the apples before putting on the top pastry, the juice would not escape.

Mary: I'll try that the next time, Peg. Thanks for the tip.

Joan: Maybe you didn't seal the edges properly Mary. Make sure you do that as well.

President: I'm sure it will be fine, Mary. Next, we have to provide cups and saucers and sandwiches. Will you look after the cups Joan?

Joan: Yes, I'll borrow them from the C Y M S, although I really like good china cups. The tea tastes much better out of them, I think.

Peg: Personally, I like a decent mug of tea. Not one of those tiny cups. C Y M S ware is good enough for me.

Mary: Talking about cups, at Birds' Bazaar this year, I won a beautiful bone china set of ware-Royal Tara with gold rims and a floral design. I wouldn't lend it to my best friend.

Peg: (aside) She wouldn't.

President: That's the china dealt with. All club members who are not on the team have kindly offered to be at the C Y M S on Sunday morning at 10 am to make sandwiches etc.

ALL: Very good.

Joan: The players can take it easy.

President: We have enough money, Joan, for ham and salad?

Joan: Plenty. We have 200 euros on hand. I hope we will have a fine day. This summer wasn't too bad, though. We went to Lanzarote for two weeks.

President: Lucky for you, Joan. Now, Peg, you are our new secretary. You will have to welcome the team: you will be good at that Peg.

Peg: Oh dear, it will be my first time. I'll be shaking in my shoes.

Mary:	You'll be fine, Peg. There's nothing to it. Just have a few notes written on a postcard. I remember being at a dinner once I don't want to digress now, Madam President, but the chairman who gave the after-dinner speech didn't have TH in his vocabulary. He went on and on about what tings de club had done during de year, tings like training de yout, tings like de lottery. Honestly, I felt like singing: 'Tinking about de tings we used to do'.
President:	Ah come on Mary. We all have faults. The important thing is that we must win on Sunday!
Joan:	Of course we'll win. We have to at home. We don't need celebrity managers, pardon me, Bainisteoiri. Our trainer is one of our own stock, as proud of the parish as any one of the team. We are proud of you Madam our President and our trainer.
President:	Thank you Joan, I know you will not let me down. And now, a word about the entertainment. The hypnotist confirmed that he is coming and guarantees that all smokers will be off cigarettes before the end of the night.
Peg:	I for one am never again going to be hypnotized. You all remember a few years ago when Paul Golden had me on stage doing Elvis singing 'Love Me Tender'. I'll never, never forget it as long as I live.
Mary:	It's often funny on the Late Late Show.
Joan:	Were ye watching the 'Late Late' last week?

BELL

President:	There's Paddy the caretaker. In five minutes time, we have to be gone out of here.
Joan:	That was a grand meeting, Madam P. Roll on Sunday.
President:	Slan abhaile, girls. See you on the pitch, Sunday at 2.30pm.

Mary Collins

The New Doctor

She arrived in the village on the first of the month and her arrival was noted when her car - a red Morris Minor - stopped at the dispensary. The driver was a woman, and sitting on the passenger seat beside the driver - a dog! What would she be like? They were so used to the old doctor, who had died a few months back, God be good to him. He knew all their ways and their ills. The men especially were gloomy. We'll see, they said to themselves, we'll see. She got out of the car and looked around. It was a pretty little village situated in the lush Tipperary countryside, surrounded by woods, which she discovered later were called the Deerpark.

In those days the dispensary was part of a dwelling-house whose owner leased a couple of rooms to the doctor. In this case there was a waiting room, an examination room and a dispensary for the doctor to make up the drugs she had prescribed. Having met the owner, who was also the district midwife, the new doctor started her day. There were few patients that morning, only the hardy vanguard, all women who would take no nonsense from a girleen young enough to be their daughter

The morning went pleasantly though it was quieter than usual, and was marked by the absence of men. These came later and were much easier to deal with than the women, except for the fact that the sight of a syringe often caused a fainting attack in the tallest and strongest looking, one of whom nearly fell on top of her. Dispensary session over, she had a call to do at the extreme edge of the district. She arrived to find a gypsy caravan, Romany type, situated at the edge of a wood beside a little stream. It was obviously new and beautifully painted, with colourful curtains and rugs. The young couple were newly married. The girl had a Madonna-like face, she was beautiful, and the young man had the dark complexion that one associates with gypsies. They were a lovely couple. They stayed in that area for over a year and the doctor saw them quite often. One day they were gone, and she never saw them again. But she often thought of them over the years and hoped that life had been kind to them. This was the first day of a very happy two years for the doctor and her dog, who became a well-known passenger. Looking back, life was slower then and less frantic, and there seemed to be time for everything. Even for a bit of gossip at the end of a consultation!

T William Powell

The Flight Of The Water Chestnuts

Even now the memory haunts me like a nutcracker to the, er, nuts. It probably always strikes readers as sheer fiction, when they become acquainted with a tale of such a lives-in-the-balance sort of story. Given that it takes place in that widely-thought harmless eastern corner of England, known sometimes as the garden of England, more usually Kent, and as it happens it's been the venue for a mind-numbing amount of sheer cant in its time.

You see, people don't think of Canterbury as the sort of spot where bloody deeds occur. As so often in life's mottled tapestry, what the eye sees or the distant mind believes, is simply out of kilter with reality.

You think Scorsese walked the streets of New York in coming up with the setting for Mean Streets? Most folk do, you're not alone. Very few realise he spent his formative years on the cobbled streets of Kent, usually Canterbury when he could pluck up the courage to walk those mean streets outside the cathedral where Thomas A-Becket lost his head. He may have been the first, but it started a local tradition. Kipling didn't just come up with his line "if you can keep your head while all around you are losing their's" by coincidence you know. Oh no, he knew the grim reality of life on those bloodied Kentish streets.

It was on the face of it a fairly ordinary day in Canterbury when this particular moment of drama, pique and bloody resolution took place. Folk reading their poems on street corners in search of enough coppers to fund their supper, more often receiving an old, stale bhaji thrown at them; or attempting to grace the atmosphere with their latest short story in hope of silver coins and so the possibility of wild celebration later that night - a cup of tea, maybe even a portion of chips - was able to appear tantalisingly before them, usually as mirage-like as the blank page just waiting to be filled with coruscating prose when they left home that morning. They'd return that night, still penniless, still seeking to cement their buttocks to the barely-standing stool by their table, upon which that old typewriter sat, just waiting for them to be able to afford another sheet of paper. Maybe the fish shop could help.

It had been an especially unrewarding day, spent out busking with stories and poems that, when the push of daylight came to the shove of facts, the hoi-polloi simply weren't up to understanding, never mind coughing up some coins in grateful appreciation of.

Bart walked back into the shop, found two customers stood there, haggling over the price of a bag of peanuts. He didn't hear the precise words they used, he was so bemused by the unremitting stupidity of the world at large that he wasn't quite hearing the words they were piping out in a nasal whine, but then he began to realise there was some sort of verbal fisticuffs going on, and so tried to pay attention.

"This bag is old and rotten. Give me another one." That was the first clear sentence he heard. Bart looked round to consider the mouth from whence these rancid words had come, and found the selfsame old wizened woman who'd not only chosen not to throw any coins his way ten minutes before as he had graciously bestowed 'Life is a bottle of acid' on the populace, but had audibly told him what a terrible piece of poetry she considered it to be.

Right, you pus on the boil of the world, thought Bart. He turned and picked up a tin of water chestnuts, held it securely in his hand, and then pitched it straight at the woman's head.

Clunk. It was such a sweet sound. The woman dropped to the floor, there was a shriek from someone, but the over-riding sense - at least in Bart's mind - was one of champagne, happiness, and justice delivered.

Hazel Endean

Watercolour Magic

Our week's painting course was drawing to a close. 15 adults from all walks of life grouped together to learn the rudiments of watercolours. Painting 'en plein air' was the order of the day. Come rain or shine, we ventured into the environs of Lisdoonvarna, armed with the necessary paraphernalia. Six cars followed our tutor's lead: onto The Burren, into the countryside, wherever he chose to take us. All week I had struggled with my skies, too many back-runs resembling exploding atom bombs. Water, very tricky; almost impossible to capture the flow. Trees? Average! As for rocks, might as well forget it!

At each studio session, I began to feel slightly inferior. James, our tutor, dismissed my efforts with a mumbled, "Very good, yes very good. Keep at it" before moving quickly to Julie alongside; where he spent a considerable amount of time guiding the brush in her hand, adding embellishments to an already perfect picture.

It wasn't just Julie. Our young Italian student, Alicia, with not a word of English, gazed admiringly into his eyes as he fawned over her sparkling angel. Where did she conjure up that one? Not the Burren, that's for sure! Every day I had filled the flasks with coffee and loaded James' car with his easel, stool, paints etc. In return, he offered me a back seat, which suited me fine, saving me the bother of driving.

By Friday I was beginning to tire. Not only were my paintings not improving, I was becoming despondent about the whole thing. Maybe watercolours were not my forté after all; perhaps I should switch to oils or acrylics. People said they were much easier to control. Then a strange thing happened on our very last day. We were sitting on The Burren, surrounded by a party of foreign tourists. My brush moved smoothly over the paper… sky, sea and rocks appeared as if by magic. It was all so perfect! The onlookers applauded - murmurs of "Bravo" and "Excellent" floated in the air. I couldn't believe it! Maybe Alicia's angel was there after all. At first, naturally, I didn't know how to react or what to say, but the picture did it for me. James, curious to know what was going on, joined me, whispering, "Very good, yes very good. Keep at it."

And I will.

Carol Clifford

Soul Search

Storm winds blow
Wild and free
Green waves crash
From a foam filled sea

Hearts will break
Crack and bleed
Minds will fly
From the pain within

He has gone
Away from me
Left my side
For the stars so deep

Weep my friend
For a soul set free
High and wild
From a foam-filled sea

Hold my hand
In a land so bare
Touch my heart
To make sure it's there

Kate Ahern

Confirmation / The Dress Of Gold

It was 1945, and here I was in bed with pleurisy and I was 12 years old. I did not have to go to hospital, the doctor said I needed a lot of rest. He gave Ma a tiny brown bottle of drops that I was to take, three times a day after meals, they always tasted awful, so I used to mix them with the end of the tea to make them more palatable. Confirmation was coming up on April 30th. Would I be allowed to receive the sacrament? Wouldn't I look a right fool if I had to wait another three and a half years? Confirmation only took place in our Parish every three years, I would be much taller then and miss out on the big occasion with my school friends. I feared that I would be down at the back with all the young people who were not allowed to go through the ceremony the previous years. They were regarded as dunces. They were stigmatised in a way that wouldn't happen today. Some of the boys wore long trousers so that they could leave school to go looking for a job. For poor families, finding work was crucial.

Preparation for the sacrament started a year beforehand. There was a small catechism, a bible history and catechism notes, a slim volume, which I nevertheless found very difficult to understand. Two pages of each had to be learnt by heart every night; woe betide anyone that missed their homework the next day. Once a fortnight, the local parish priest examined us on our religious knowledge. You had to speak out in a clear voice and put your hand up and if questioned by him you had to answer right or wrong. He got really annoyed if the pupils mumbled their answers. Some children were so frightened they were struck dumb even when they knew the answer! We didn't understand a lot of the Catechism, words like transubstantiation were a mystery to most of us. The girls in the other classes would have gone through the text before. Sometimes we found the Bible history confusing, so there was a lot of worry that we would miss our religious questions on Confirmation day in the Church.

There was excitement too as we thought of new dresses and being the centre of attention on our big day. Everybody was relieved when our Parish priest, a cranky, impatient man, was replaced a month before Confirmation. The new priest was kind, friendly and easy-going. Rev. Mother had a chat with him and after Ma had got permission from the doctor so that I could receive the sacrament without having to sit in the Church for an hour, I was questioned instead in the school for ten minutes on my religious knowledge by the new priest. After a year of intense preparation, my fears vanished as the questions seemed so simple after all the worry and torment.

As time was short the next big task for Ma was to buy the dress for the big day. Father had died the previous year so money was very scarce, but Ma always rose to the occasion. She had a great eye for colour and style and was always on the lookout for a bargain. We scanned the Irish Press. One day there was a picture of a lovely dress made of taffeta available in three colours: pale pink, blue and old-gold. It was priced 29s/11d post paid from Kelletts of George's Street in Dublin. The only drawback was that it had short puff sleeves. A jacket or coat would have to be worn over it, as I would have to be kept very warm so as not to have a relapse.

Ma sent off the postal order to Kelletts. We watched for the postman every day and when the parcel arrived what excitement and delight we had! When we opened the box it revealed the old gold dress wrapped in white tissue paper and a receipt and compliments of the firm on the bottom. My dream had come true.

The doctor had allowed me to attend the ceremony on the big day. My older brothers had sent me shoes. From Tim, a pair of black patent size 4 shoes in the post and Pat, a pair of brown brogues. As I was Pat's favourite I decided to wear the brown ones. My youngest brother Arthur carried me on the bar of his bike before the ceremony. The lady of the house where he worked made lovely hot buttered toast and tea for me. Then up to the church to sit with my friends and receive the blessing and strength of the Holy Spirit.

The village was decorated with bunting, and the gold and white papal flag hung outside the church. It was a great occasion, the choir was there in force, the local pipe band played 'Faith of our Fathers', and the LDF provided the guard of honour and a salute for his Lordship. One of the top brass in the force shook hands with the Bishop instead of kneeling and kissing his ring, as was the custom then. It was the talk of the village for days afterwards.

I felt strengthened by the pat on the cheek and being blessed by the Bishop with the holy oil on my forehead. Ma was so happy and proud that I was confirmed; I was the youngest of nine. My family was so delighted that I was getting my health and strength back.

Mary Collins

The Pound Note

I was born, so to speak, in the Central Bank and though I was one of many thousands, I was unique because I had a special number which distinguished me from the rest of my companions.

I had a rather attractive appearance, with Lady Lavery on one side and the Ploughman on the other. I was dispatched rather quickly to one of the various banks around Dublin and there I sat waiting for my new owner. She was a middle-aged lady who remarked on my beauty, which straight away endeared her to me. She however parted with me very quickly, which disappointed me, as I had a rather nice resting place in her designer handbag.

I now found myself in a cash drawer in Brown Thomas with a motley crowd of notes, but I was still unique and still in a pristine condition. Later in the day I was given out in change to a young man buying a rather jazzy scarf. He was on his way to meet his girlfriend and I think he hoped the scarf would make a good impression - it did. Soon after, I was pushed across the counter of a bar in exchange for a gin and tonic. The drawer in which I now found myself was rather a comedown. My fellow notes were rather a tatty crowd and told stories of having been at the races. They were on the whole tired-looking and sadly worn at the edges - they were, however, good company and entertained me with funny yarns about their former owners, which made a pleasant change from a rather dull life so far.

That evening we were all shifted to the bank and I for one enjoyed the overnight stay and rest which I badly needed. After that I did various jaunts around the city, nothing very interesting, but alas I finished up in the pocket of a very drunk man who dropped me out of his pocket as he shambled along - and there was I, wet and dirty in the gutter! What a sad end to a wonderful beginning. The wind blew me along and I got stuck in someone's shoe. It was a young woman with a baby in her arms. She looked down and saw me and picked me up lovingly, and carefully dried me on her coat, and her eyes shone brightly through the tears as she looked at the sky and thanked God. Now she had food for her baby and herself. As for me, was there a better way to go out of circulation?

Carol Clifford

Listen

Let me tell you the truth. Not the lies of politicians to further their own aims but the truth as I and the others lived it. This colony was founded, not on kingly glory, but on poverty, starvation and fear.

My father was well born, a civic counsellor with land and many slaves. My mother governed her household with a generous hand. As the eldest son I was taught the responsibilities owed to my family and people. But these did not weigh too heavily on my shoulders and I ran free as other boys over the mountains and sands of Thera, my island home. We rambled through the olive groves and when our energy was spent we lay beneath the lemon trees with their sweet sharp scent resting on the still air. When thirsty, we could persuade sheep or goats with our nimble fingers to disgorge their sun warmed sweetness straight into our waiting mouths. Such was my life.

On reaching manhood a marriage was arranged within a neighbouring family. Eleni and I had played in childhood until she was enfolded into the secret women's world behind the closed doors of her mother's kitchen. She now entered our house as a bride. It was a good match and we were happy. The first dark omen of things to come was the unexpected death of my father, leaving the care of my mother and two young brothers in my hands. That same year saw the crops fail for the first time in my memory. But the storehouses were full and no one went hungry. Little did we guess of the horrors to come. For the next five years our land yielded naught but barren crops and rotting fruit. The fish had deserted our bays and inlets, the boats losing their bright blue sheen to the harsh hot dust of the gods' anger. In the seventh year even the sacred olive trees dropped their hard unripened fruit onto the dry brown earth. Many people did not live to see this last disaster. Newly weaned infants went first, their mother's milk no longer flowing. The old ones went next, with their wisdom lost to us for evermore. My mother, no longer able even to drink the earth flavoured soup, joined her husband in his tomb. Harder yet to bear was the birth of our first born child, destroying his weakened mother with his urge to see light, that light so quickly quenched.   I buried them with my parents.

When the grumbling God's anger overflowed, with fiery rivers flowing through channels newly formed by his volcanic outburst, the Council in desperation begged help from our ancient oracle. How had we offended the gods so much that this had descended on us? The reply came - go to Cyrene and found a colony. Where was Cyrene? No one knew, so no one went.

Darkness fell on our land again. The graveyards grew, spilling over into the orange groves, formerly as rich and bright as the evening sun; now their rotting fruit gave nourishment to the barren ground. We starved and saw our children die.

We again consulted the oracle and again the answer came - go to Cyrene and found a colony. This time it was heeded and the decision was made to send three fifty-oared ships across the unknown sea to seek out this promised land. The rowers would be picked by lot, one out of every three males in a household. I was the one chosen from our house, leaving my brothers with a chance of life if our fields yielded again. We must never return home for the Gods might, in anger, take out our disobedience on the remaining families. So I left my home, my brothers and the graves of my future. My parents had taught me well my responsibilities. My thoughts whilst pulling on the oars away from that much-loved land remained in my breast. Only to you, my grandson will my heart be open and only to you, who cherish truth, will my story and that of Cyrene be told.

Hazel Endean

Roses

Dawn broke slowly over the rose garden, the birds' chorus heralding the beginning of a soft warm day.

Against the mellow stone walls, the flesh- pink blooms 'Irish Mist' and 'New Dawn' opened their petals to the pale sun. 'Fragrant Cloud' and 'Golden Showers' provided a gold and flame-red carpet at their feet.

Bordering the paved paths, the hybrids nestled alongside each other's foliage and in their beds, the miniature roses 'Yellow Doll' and 'Baby Masquerade' slept peacefully. Yesterday, this haven of quiet beauty had been disrupted by the arrival of a new rose, 'Queen Elizabeth'. Annoyed at having been uprooted from its palatial home, it considered a Garden for the Blind definitely a come-down in life. Holding heads in the air, they said; "Visitors won't see our beauty and perfection; we will be wasted here."

Pale-yellow 'Peace' spoke softly. "You should feel honoured to be here. Where you came from, did anyone caress your velvet petals with love and reverence? Did they smell your exquisite perfume with a sense of wonder and awe? The rest of us would not wish to be anywhere else but here, in God's own garden. Your beauty will be appreciated as never before, and in time, when your roots are firmly settled, you will be glad you came."

Over the whole garden came a hushed whisper as heads nodded in agreement.

Hazel Endean

Myrtle

It all started when I was planning a foreign holiday with my friend Mary. We hadn't seen much of each other for a while so it seemed a good idea at the time. Having been friends all our lives we knew each other inside out, so when she proposed inviting her sister-in-law Myrtle to join us, I felt slightly ill at ease.

Myrtle had recently lost her husband; it would do her good to get away, Mary said. Of course she had to go with us, but I began to doubt if this trio would work. Mary and I shared the same sense of humour; most of our time we giggled and joked between ourselves. Somehow I couldn't see Myrtle joining in; she was a dour lady who rarely smiled. That was when she had everything going for her; now, recently widowed, there was no chance. Her very name wasn't conducive to hilarity! What kind of mother would call her daughter 'Myrtle' for goodness sake? (Sincere apologies to any Myrtles out there, by the way). Mind you, my name isn't much better, but I do know how to have a good time. I mix well, get on with everyone I meet and always have a store of jokes to tell if the atmosphere gets somewhat chilly. (The one about the balloon works every time; they fall about laughing at that one). Anyway, being a charitable person, I was determined to bring a smile to Myrtle's face even if it killed me.

We swam, shopped, walked, ate delicious food, went sight-seeing; it was hard work but I had to get that woman to smile. We flirted, danced, laughed and drank but poor Myrtle found it hard to join in. She declined the hotel's evening entertainment, feigning headaches and grief. Even my balloon joke had no effect on her at all. So eventually I gave up, I was wasting valuable time; there were others who greatly appreciated my bonhomie. Our holiday was fast coming to an end and we had to make the most of the time available, so we left poor Myrtle to her own devices.

On our last night, we partied with abandon. I'm afraid we had too many piña coladas, so decided to retire earlier than intended. As we stumbled out of the lift, we were shocked to see a bikini-clad woman tiptoeing towards the large broom cupboard on our landing. Was it an illusion? Were we so addled with drink? We looked at each other, both of us gobsmacked and speechless. A bronzed arm shot out and the vision of Myrtle disappeared from view. Well, we all like to let our hair down when away from home, but this? Falling onto our ruffled beds we stared at the empty one, so immaculately kept not a single crease to be seen. In unison, we raised an imaginary glass to the absent Myrtle: "Cheers! See ya in the morning. Go for it you devil!" We collapsed into our duvets, tears rolling down our cheeks. Maybe it was the drink or were we a little envious of the 'Not so poor Myrtle' after all? By the way, I never got around to telling you the one about the balloon did I? Have you got half an hour to spare?

Jack O'Dwyer

Ghost Stories

Long ago, ghost stories were quite common. People would tell them for hours and hours every night. In the days before television, when people had only oil lamps or candles for lighting up the room and the old turf fire for heating, weird shadows would be seen flitting across the white washed walls; the ceilings would come alive. Children would be frightened when the story teller would relate what he claimed to have heard outside the house.

The man of the house would go out maybe to bring in a bucket of turf and hear sounds in the darkness; a lone dog barking, footsteps round the gable end, rustling in the bushes. People had vivid imaginations, and could be convinced of the presence of a ghost when passing a big house with the high walls casting shadows all around. The whistling of high wind in the tall trees gave rise to belief in the banshee who wailed when a death was about to occur.

I remember cycling home very late one dark night. I had no lamp on my bike. There was a small wood which made the road even darker, when suddenly I saw some large object moving in the middle of the road. I immediately thought of a ghost and jumped off my bike in fright, a cold shiver coming over me. In panic, I remounted to cycle back to where I had come from. However, I still felt I had to get home even though I would have to face my ghost again. I soon discovered that this large moving object was nothing more than a big black donkey rolling in the dust, enjoying himself having a good old stretch.

When I turned the next corner, I could see the lights of town in the distance. I at once felt safe, no longer in fear of the harmless ghost. But, a hundred yards from home what should I see? Another big black form coming towards me! My heart nearly stopped when a burly Garda demanded, "Where is your bicycle lamp?"

Mick Jones

A Normal Tuesday Evening

It was a normal Tuesday evening, with the normal family row about which programme to watch. Mum wanted Coronation Street, because of all the advertising about the latest unexpected twist in the story line. Dad wanted the preview of the rugby match between Ireland & Scotland. Jim wanted the special double episode of The Simpsons, and Leticia wanted the final of America's Next Top Model.

It was more or less the same every Tuesday. The programmes were sometimes slightly different, sometimes the boys argued against the girls; sometimes the adults squabbled with the children. The two consistent things were the lack of agreement between them and the constant battle to control the zapper. It was just about five to seven, and the arguments, leg pulling, yelling and teasing were reaching the point when Dad usually said enough was enough, when Jimmy shouted out.

"Dad, look! Shut up and look, please!"

The adverts had been interrupted by a broadcast that no one recognised. The screen was a fuzzy black and white, and an old woman was speaking. The whole family sat, eyes and mouths wide open. No one had changed channel, the zapper was on the floor under the coffee table where Dad had thrown it a couple of minutes ago.

"Can you hear me?" The voice was muffled, but the determination behind the words was unmistakable. "Get out of the house, and go now!"

"Is this a prank or…" Dad started to ask Jimmy, but Jimmy's focus was fixed on the TV.

"Dad, please, shut up and listen, please Dad."

The urgent tone in his son's voice made Dad feel this was not some kind of prank, but just maybe it was one of those TV stunts. They could be very realistic and convincing. "Jim, it's some kind of hoax, don't get scared, you know what these TV people get up to, don't worry…"

The old lady kept repeating the same thing over and over, just getting more insistent. "Get out, go now!"

"Dad, please…" Jimmy was in no mind to be reassured by his Dad, "we have to do what she says, get out of the house. Please let's go now, Dad please!"

"Jim, it will be fine, calm down there's nothing to be…"

Then, a sound like an explosion, though that's not what it was. The family was stunned into silence. They carefully got up out of their sofas and looked out of the window. The back yard was full of rubble, and in the middle, the unmistakable wreckage of the chimney pot.

"Dad, can we go outside please, I'm scared."

They all trooped out into the garden to view the wrecked roof, it seemed as though the chimney had just collapsed for no good reason. Whatever and however, there was now a gaping hole in their roof.

"Dad, you remember when the dog got run over, I told you a lady on the telly had told me to keep her in the kennel that night. It was the same lady. Dad I'm not joking, you all saw her this time!"

T William Powell

Last Night

The night was so incredibly beautiful, but all I saw were the ruby drops in the snow, and the broken wings of the murdered angel. I followed the drops to the corner of the lake, where I saw a feather or two more - could they be more of the broken wings? I didn't know, but I felt they probably were.

It had been such a strange night all round, the switching of the elements from warm and sunny - here in December mind you - too cold, very cold, and swirling wind and snow. And then just a short time back, maybe twenty minutes, it had felt warm again, warm as the winter evening drew in, and beautiful was the only word to accurately describe the night that was now here. That sunset… set against the bright white snow surrounds and the contrasting night against white that the falling sun, the depth of snow, and the brightness with the falling dark created. And then I saw the ruby drops.

Like the sun almost set and the snow in the dark, the drops of ruby red nestling with rich and unsettling clarity in the pure white snow made a startling poles apart, yet set together scene. I think it was because I was still trying to get my head around such a clear, yet at the same time hard to believe, striking contrast that it was the ruby drops I noticed first; it must have been a minute or so before I noticed the broken wings.

What was happening here? The scarcely feasible warmth of a December night, the crystal clear white of the fallen snow, the violent discovery of ruby drops - they had to be blood, didn't they? - and now broken wings, and what was that further on, up towards the lake?

I'd walked there and seen what appeared to be a straggled few feathers, and so what was this? A murdered angel. There it lay, the remnants of the rest of it, minus wings, with big, ugly splashes of ruby red blood across the corpse of the murdered angel. Had I ever seen such a heart-rending sight? An angel, bloodily murdered… what a dismal way to mark the festive season.

And then it struck me - hold on, an angel, murdered? But surely angels are not of this cold and dank world at all, how can it be that an angel could be murdered? Wouldn't that be the killing of 'life' from the other world? The killing of the already dead?

I had entered a curious state of mind right enough; here I was, by the lake where I'd thought I would take a stroll on such a striking night as Christmas approached, yet it felt like I was somewhere removed from the home I'd walked out of not more than a few minutes ago. Drops of unmistakably blood in the snow, broken wings from an angel, and then the rest of the angel's body, what was going on? Was I in some sort of netherworld? Had I drunk too much and wandered into a dream-like subconscious nightmare while I walked to the lake?

So many questions, I lacked any answers though. Except I realised then that no, I hadn't drunk anything stronger than a cup of coffee before I headed out to the lake, that was why I set out to walk then, to take in the remarkable beauty of this night before closing the door and supping a festive bevy or two. I was now feeling very woozy in the head, all the more so having recognised that no, I hadn't taken a single shot of whisky before this walk.

I threw my face upwards, closed my eyes and took a deep breath. When I ran my hands back down my face, the night was still dark, the snow was still clear white and beautiful, and I looked back down at the angel body, except it wasn't there. I hurried over to where I'd seen the broken wings, and there was nothing there either. The drops of blood, they must still be here I thought, but no, I looked all around and there were none. Then, as I was struggling to comprehend what on earth was going on, what had gone on, to try and make some sort of order of what felt like the most bizarre and unnerving night of my life, these voices suddenly came out of the darkness,

"God rest ye merry gentleman, let nothing you dismay", it sounded like a choir, like a whole host of voices singing this Christmas carol,

"God rest ye merry gentleman, let nothing you dismay", again, and then "God rest ye merry gentleman, let nothing you dismay" once more, and so it continued, just that one line. It took hearing it sung by the choir several times for me to realise: they were singing gentle*man* not men and now I felt all the more confused, scared and utterly unsure as to whether this was me dreaming the most distorted dream or what else was causing this bemusing and senses-addling state of mind and being.

The singing of "God rest ye merry gentleman" continued, sounding like a choir of many, and yet I saw absolutely nobody. What was this? I had no idea what was taking place. I went to the lake, but there was nothing to see there. The angel corpse was no longer there, just as the angel wings had disappeared, the ruby drops of blood had gone as well. Then I turned around and there stood the angel, the same angel I'd seen before because she was spattered with ruby drops and she was holding her broken wings in her arms. She was stood with her back to me, but she turned then, and now my incomprehension and utter shock reached a new level - it was Margaret. The murdered angel, holding her broken wings in front of her, was my dear departed wife; Margaret, who had died three years before. The choir's singing faded now, not that I had ever seen them at all, and there stood Margaret, smiling at me in her blood-spattered angelic form. I had to wake up now, surely. But I didn't, I just heard the choir singing "God rest ye merry gentleman" in the background, and had the completely impossible yet wonderful visitation of my dead wife in front of me.

"Come, my darling, come now. It is time." she said, as she stretched out her hand to me. I tried to hold it, but there was nothing to feel when I did so.

"Come darling, we can meet again now" said she, as she continued to stretch her hands out to me, continued to smile while being decked in blood, her broken wings having dropped to the ground as she reached out to me. I remembered - how would I ever forget? - how Margaret had died at the hands of a murderer, how there had been drops of blood from where she lay to the lake, how I had felt I would never get over the brutal death of my wife that day, and then I remembered too how I had, just before taking my walk outside on such a beautiful night, picked up the pills and tipped them all into my hand.

"Come my darling, it is time now."

Mick Jones

The House Down The Road From Us

(A childhood poem revisited)

A house of ivy and brick
Of ghost stories, tragic and true
Ice cold in December, deep frozen in May
It is black by night and blacker by day,
And for years the house has stood that way.

I would never go in that house you know
And no-one I know, has dared to go
For that house is alive and murderous too
For I've heard it said that those who do
Cross the threshold are lost from view

So many tales are told and retold
Of hapless innocent disappeared souls
The sinister whispers from absence of breath,
Uncertainty subtly ushers in death;
An insatiable malice that lingers there yet

But alas, poor house, I pity you now.
For your days are over,
Your punishment death,
Bulldozers wait at the gate
Men arriving with shovels and picks
For you there can be no escape

Jimmy, this bulldozer won't start!
Jimmy!
Jimmy?

Jo Scanlon

Fly Through The Keyhole

Long, long ago, when I was a child, the village story-teller Sean used to enthral all of us children with his scary tales. Will he ever start, we would wonder. We knew he often went up the mountain for a day's shooting, taking home a big bag of pheasants. One day after a good shoot, as he gathered up his bag and his gun, a sudden thick mist came down all round him. Sean was not the least bit frightened, as this had often happened before, only to lift after some time. He sat on a rock to take a rest before descending, but the fog was getting worse and worse, and darkness seemed to have fallen. I have to go, he thought, as he stood up and peered through the blanket of fog, hoping to see some sign of light.

He proceeded very slowly and cautiously over the stony surface, picking his way by feeling for boulders and rocks. He was soon really and truly frightened, when thankfully, he saw a glimmer of light in the distance piercing the thick fog. After some time, with a sigh of relief he picked out lamplight. Finally he could see, quite near him now, a house with lights shining through every window. As he drew nearer, he could hear sounds of music and merriment.

Thank God, he thought as he rushed to the door and banged loudly on the brass knocker. The door opened at once. There standing on the threshold was an old hag with red watery eyes and wearing a gaudy tattered shawl. "Come in," she said, "we will give you something to eat." He came into a large room filled with dancers and musicians. They took not the slightest notice of Sean as they danced wildly and noisily.

The old witch pointed him to a vacant chair and went away. Almost at once a second uglier hag appeared carrying a plate of bread and meat. As he sat greedily eating, the third and by far the most forbidding looking of the three was standing in the middle of the floor, her mane of jet black greasy hair hanging down to her waist and almost covering her face. With an ugly scowl, she clapped her hands and at once there was silence. "It is the midnight hour," she shouted, "the time for everyone to leave!" In a flash they were all gone except for Sean and the three witches. "You cannot go to your home to-night," croaked the black haired one. "You are staying here until daylight." Suddenly all the lights went out as she handed Sean a lighted candle, and showed him in to a room, warning him to quench the candle before going to bed.

The poor man, out of his wits with fear, did not know what to do. He lay fully dressed under the bedclothes, too terrified to sleep. After what seemed like hours, he heard the door opening slowly, and even with his eyes shut tight he could feel the light of the candle approaching his bed. After assuring herself that he was asleep, the first witch went to a press in the wall. Sean dared to open an eye and saw her taking something out of the press and putting it on her head half-singing, half-chanting, "Little red cap, fly through the keyhole" and away she went.

Sean hardly had time to think when witch number two came in, repeating the same black magic. She too disappeared. When the ugliest hag entered, Sean was numb with terror as he listened to the hoarse voice intoning, "Little red cap, fly through the keyhole." As soon as she had gone off, Sean decided that he was not going to spend the rest of the night in that place of evil. "I must do something!" he muttered. He took out his box of matches, lit the candle and found the press still almost full of red caps. Quickly taking one he put it on his head, quenched the candle and nervously but hopefully recited the formula: "Little red cap, fly through the keyhole."

In less than no time, he opened his eyes to find himself lying on the ground beside a large building very familiar to him. The countryside around was noted for apple growing and this old storehouse was where the cider was made. Only one window showed light and Sean ran over, afraid no more. He peeped in to see the most revolting of spectacles. There were the three witches wildly waving bottles of cider, singing raucously, or croaking with laughter. Taking another look he saw the three little caps thrown on a chair. He ran like lightning to the Garda barracks. "Now we know," said one of the guards, when they heard the story "who has been stealing all our cider." They raced to the old store, broke in through another window and caught the three witches red handed just as they were making for the chair to retrieve their caps. For all I know, they are still in jail.

Mary Collins

Ghosts At Home

In the late 1990s my husband, self and our two children returned to Ireland. We had spent four years in the U.S.A. and enjoyed the experience but now had to test the strength of the Celtic Tiger and let's face it, we had become nostalgic and our children had become bored with listening to the 'what if's'. We arrived on a beautiful spring day, which augured well for our hopes of a nice house. We stayed with relatives who welcomed us with open arms and started our search. It wasn't as easy as our hopes led us to believe. We spent day after day driving round the Meath countryside, looking for our dream house. We arrived back at evening time, tired and dispirited and felt that the welcome mat was getting a bit threadbare! Then, a day of hope - we heard of an old house situated on the banks of the Boyne. It had been a landlord's house in the old days and was now empty.

So we started out to see it, our hopes rekindled. It was situated in a sunny valley not far from the famous river, surrounded by a field of daffodils. We discovered it was about two hundred years old; one of the last of the landlords' residences. It was absolutely beautiful and even before seeing it properly, we fell in love with it. It was Georgian in style, with long floor-to-ceiling windows looking out on the river. It sat in about four acres, with stables and two orchards. It had absolutely no 'mod cons'; water was piped to the house from a spring well and definitely no central heating. Strange to say, during the four years we spent there, we never missed it. There were fireplaces in every room and one could fit a big log in any one of them. The kitchen was in the basement, with an antediluvian range. We decided to scrap that and turn the dining room into an open plan kitchen / dining room.

There were four bedrooms facing south, so we had plenty of room and when our furniture was delivered it suited the house. We settled in quickly and happily.

Whilst there, we survived the tail-end of a hurricane. The wind and rain lashed against our windows and all the trees in the avenue were knocked down. The village, which was situated on a hill, had all its roofs blown off, but we didn't lose a slate! We walked to the village the morning after and people thought we were ghosts; they had decided that we hadn't a hope of surviving. But the ghosts were to come!

Although we were happy there, we eventually decided to move to a big town. The children were growing up and needed secondary education, so very regretfully we had to leave.

In the final week of our stay, strange things began to happen. My husband had gone ahead to sort out a suitable home and school and I was alone with my children. Having retired to bed at the usual time, I was wakened by the sound of footsteps running up and down the corridor between the bedrooms. For some reason I opened the door of my bedroom and a sudden gust of wind banged it shut. I sat up in terror until dawn broke. The following night there was a repeat of the footsteps and this was added to by the sound of saucepans being thrown about - my room was above the kitchen. All this continued until the day we were leaving; I had a feeling that the spirits didn't want us to leave. On the final night I knelt down and prayed for their souls and told them I loved the house and hated leaving.

Some years later the house was sold to a builder. I heard they had found a cellar that we didn't know existed underneath the passage in the old kitchen. In it were found human bones and chains.

We used to call down to see the house whenever we were passing and heard that the builder and his mates had left suddenly and never finished the job. Happily the house was eventually completed and looked beautiful in the afternoon sun. Many years later I told the story of the house to my children. They were so cross that I hadn't told them at the time. We later discovered that in spite of the refurbishment the house has never been lived in since.

Mick Jones

Restless In The Reeks

I'd climbed and rambled through the Reeks since I was in my late teens. I'd learnt the hard ways and safe places, the soft landings and the 'traps' to avoid at all cost. Many times I'd been stranded by fog or sleet and forced to wait the weather out. Not only that, but by the time you have two boys in their twenties (as I did) you learn to be aware of your own limitations as well. Of course, there were plenty of serious climbers and ramblers with knowledge and skills far greater than mine, but these beautiful, treacherous rocks were as much in my blood as the oxygen we breathe. More than a second home you might say, almost… a sanctuary.

I tended to avoid the Devil's ladder as a route up Carantouhill, too 'touristy' for my tastes. Probably sounds a bit snobby, but I had favourite routes of my own, not all of them in the guidebooks. Generally, I went the long way round, via Caher. Caher is a 'softer' route to the Carantouhill summit, but with loads of inviting variations. Some simply providing a feast for the eye, privileges shared by only a few, others offering some more serious climbing challenges. There is only one way up the Devil's ladder!

There are two gullies on the south side of Caher. One that I often use brings you to a steady but exhilarating scramble towards the last path up the ridge which, in turn, leads on to Carrantouhill. The other seems to lead nowhere, but after some exploration over the years, I found it leads to a hidden lake, black in deep shadow, and a few insignificant looking caves. Some of the regular climbers had mentioned this as a dead end, and no one I knew had anything interesting to say about it.

One particularly sunny day, I decided I would take another careful look at the path that seems to lead to nowhere in particular. There are two rocks which almost form a doorway to this obscure gully and as I went through, I noticed an immediate change in the atmosphere. Not dampness, nothing odd about the wind, which was a light enough breeze anyway, but something I hadn't noticed before in all my days on these rocky slopes. There was something like sound, but nothing musical to compare it with. This was a low frequency vibration, which seemed to be in my gut more than in my ears. I had an anxious moment wondering about quakes, but then noticed that whatever the vibration was, it seemed quite steady. This wasn't a rumble, because you couldn't really hear it and anyway, rumbles change pitch and intensity. Rumbles are not constant. I walked slowly forward toward the small black lake looking round for some source of the mysterious sensation. Nothing! Wind across cave mouths I wondered. No, again, this vibration wasn't really something you could 'hear' exactly. It was just… there! I stood still, trying to pinpoint where it came from. I didn't feel afraid… but I did wonder whether I should be.

I looked around the entrances to the caves. This was a pretty dull place to be. No wonder there was little enthusiasm about this gully. I decided to take a few digital snap shots. I leant against a huge boulder to steady myself, and then something remarkable and chilling happened. The vibrations intensified. I wasn't hearing voices exactly, but my own gut seemed to be speaking to me. I jumped away from the rock as if it had bitten me, and then laughed at the absurdity of my own reaction. The laughter eased the tension briefly. I leant back on the rock to steady the camera again, but this time I felt a totally different sensation; as if I were magnetized, drawn to the rock itself. Still no sound as such, but the vibration strengthened. My stomach almost shook. Next moment, I became truly frightened. Something unusual was happening to me… no, something extraordinarily bizarre and quite terrifying was happening. Something or somebody was trying to 'speak' to me. For some reason I closed my eyes. Words seemed to be seeping into my head, though I could not work out from where. It was not an airborne sound, I was certainly not of the religious persuasion to think I might be having a vision; and I was pretty sure my state of mind wasn't that disturbed. Some of my mates say I cracked up years ago, so I wondered if it might be happening a second time! Then as I tried to move away from the stone again, a frightening realisation dawned. I was actually stuck to the huge rock. But boulders aren't magnetic. How could I be pinned to a rock? Then, from somewhere… three distinct words.

"How… could… you?"

Whatever this was, it was not part of a guilty conscience or work pressures. I was never given to hallucinations. I never did drugs, climbing was all the buzz I ever needed, and I wasn't dehydrated or anything. No, this was different… something new to me.

"How… could… you?"

The question persisted, and I was still somehow fixed to the huge rock.

"Not… you! Your… people!"

"My people?" I thought I hadn't spoken, but a reply came.

"Yes, your people! We… we despise you."

"Who are you?"

"I am no-one. Not of your kind, nor of my own…"

It made no sense. There was a pause…

"I am…" the thought seemed to trail away, and then another pause.

"Wait… do not… run."

I fell away from the rock. Whatever had kept me glued to the boulder had now released me. I had been asked not to run. It seemed best not to. For Christ's sake, I thought. Have you gone crazy? Why would you be bothered by your imagination going a bit wild? It happens sometimes! Everybody has vivid daydreams occasionally, so just get your head straight. My cautious attitude to the Reeks had earned me the nickname Captain Sensible in some quarters. Brigadier Bonkers would have seemed more apt at that moment. Then it started again.

"Do not run, you must speak with me. You should have shame, but you need not have fear."

Still no sound. Again, I briefly struggled with the question of my own sanity, but then followed a moment of true terror. The rock moved! It didn't roll or crack; it flexed itself, went still again for a moment, then distorted grotesquely… and unwound itself into a moving granite biped. The shape was vague, but unmistakably humanoid.

"Follow. You need to listen. You need to understand."

I couldn't argue with that. And given that this impossible conversation was being held with a moving lump of rock three feet taller than I was, arguing wasn't really presenting itself as an option.

"Follow."

It walked... no, staggered slowly towards the caves. I followed at a distance. It did not look back. Somehow, I sensed it didn't need to. Somehow, it knew I was following. Fifty metres on, we were at a cave. The mobile granite put its version of a hand to the side of the cave mouth. I had been terrified already, but now I completely froze. The rock opening grew wider and taller in front of my very eyes.

"Follow."

It went inside. Somehow, I regained control of my limbs, and did as asked.

"Sit. I am tired."

I sat, numb with fear. I'd been in some very dodgy situations from time to time and felt that coolness was the best way to deal with danger. But I had no idea what was happening here. I was as close to panic as I had ever been.

"Who are you?" I said, trying to fight off the growing sense of despair.

"I am no-one. I am... the remaining."

"The remaining what? I don't understand. Who are you? How can I hear you?"

"I do not know how. We do not need to know how. You need to know about my people. There are so few of us... remaining. I am very tired. My future may not be as I am now. Please be still. Your words are strange to me. Thousands of suns have passed since I last spoke to one of your kind. When I spoke, he ran. Please be still."

The vibration I felt when I first started down the path to these caves was back with greater intensity than ever. I kept still as asked. The vibration shook my gut again; it surged upward through my chest and shoulders, my head started to pound. Briefly, I felt as though I was in an earthquake. Then stillness... absolute stillness.

"Your words are strange to me, but then our races never really understood each other."

I managed a nervous question, "I have no understanding at all, what race are you?" In the stillness, there was a new calmness. I was still close to panic, but I was fighting to stay in control. The calmness helped ever so slightly.

"I am not, but my people were crystallines. Your word might be metamorphic."

"You mean people, a race that changed shape like you did? I don't understand this at all. You say your people? So are you a crystalline?"

"No, I am… remaining. When your race… dies, do their thoughts… remain?"

"Oh my God!" I couldn't help myself. My voice quavered as I spoke. "You're a ghost!"

"Ghost?" There was a long pause, "Maybe... more like a ghost of a ghost. I am memory; memory that never fades. But now, so much time has passed, even we are fading. It seems that maybe even 'never' has an ending. I am very tired."

I couldn't help agreeing that there were more important things to discuss than definitions. And I was beginning to sense that whatever I had encountered might be about to die, maybe not for the first time!

"Are you dying?"

"I am not living, but I am not alone. We are only remaining. Please, listen. You must understand what your people did." I realised I was not helping by trying to work out what this thing was. It had a message. I needed to listen. And as I finally worked that out… it knew!

"My people were crystallines. They had no… blood like you, but they did have great wisdom. They were… gentle. They did not try to 'possess' the land as your race does. They cared for the land. Millions of suns have passed now, but there was a time when both our races lived together. The crystallines were gentle, you… humans? Yes, humans, you were cruel. Worse, you enjoyed cruelty. My people could not understand. My people were born of the mountains. Their bodies were...like jewels and they lived at peace with one another. Your people feared them, but only because they feared themselves. They feared their own race, they feared each other! My people cherished the trees and grasses. They lived with the animals. They did not hunt them. Your people allowed their cruelty to rule their hearts. They drove my people back into the mountains. Often they destroyed them before they could reach safety. Some crystallines tried to fight, but we - they knew nothing of fighting, and were beaten again and again. You should be ashamed of what your fathers did to my people. It is forgotten by your kind. But we, the remaining… we remain to try to make sure that your children do not live in ignorance of their cruel fathers. You must bring this knowledge to your kind."

"But we have experts who know the history of creatures on this planet. This is nonsense, what you are saying."

"No, not nonsense. Remember, my people were crystallines. When their bodies broke, they became pebbles and dust. Maybe…experts do not know as much as they think they know. Shame often hides the truth. Over so much time, shame itself may be hidden. For your race it is time to re-awaken both shame and truth. You must do this to repay the evil of your own race. You must re-awaken the memory of my race. It is a debt that must be repaid. The sons of your race must know that your fathers killed all my people."

"ALL of your people?"

"Yes, it is true, but so long ago, it is forgotten. But truth forgotten does not change. Truth is only lost from thought until remembered again. Now is the time to remember."

"My people will think I am a madman." This solemn charge was completely beyond my imagination. I just had to survive this bizarre event, work out why I was hallucinating, and then rest until the memory faded.

"You will not forget." It seemed to know my thoughts, "You understand the importance of my words. You are a man who needs truth. You will not be able to… pretend. Even after all this time, you will find a way to re-awaken the memory. You will find a way."

Then I heard shouting and running feet, men's voices, but an unknown primitive language, the sounds of rock against rock. I was being given an action replay of a long forgotten genocide. I was being shown an evil brutality from the very dawn of pre-history. I felt myself shaking with rage, I shook helplessly for countless minutes, the sounds of violence ripped through my head. I came close to vomiting… not once, but four or five times… and then suddenly, it stopped. I found myself weeping.

"Go now. You will not forget."

As I came out of the cave, I saw the sun was beginning to set. I was in shock, but somehow I would have to gather all my concentration to get off the mountains safely that night. Never in my life before had I felt the need to escape from my beloved Reeks.

The following morning, after fitful sleep, I woke early. The previous day's events were still sharp and clear in my mind. I needed coffee! As the kettle boiled, there was a knock on the door. It was Dylan, my eldest.

"Dylan, come in, come in. Coffee?"

"Thanks Dad, perfect!" He paused, "Dad, are you OK? You look terrible!"

Dylan had a Masters degree in archaeology, so I just had to share my bizarre experience with him. But as I got deeper into the story, I sensed I had made a mistake. He clearly didn't believe me, but neither did he want to aggravate me by disagreeing. Well of course, he's a scientist; I should have prepared the ground much more carefully. But the damage was done. He was upset, but determined not to show it. I knew now that I had to shut up… anything I said would only make matters worse.

I decided I should keep my own counsel for a while, but after weeks of fretting, I felt I had to find a way to broach the subject again. Again, it seemed I got it wrong. After listening carefully for a while, Dylan put his arm round me. "Don't worry about it Dad, we'll look after you whatever happens." He always reminded me so much of his mother. She had died in a car crash ten years earlier. There was a difference though. Dylan's mum would have listened to me, however barmy I sounded.

Later on, something similar happened with Callum, my other son. He's a schoolteacher specialising in Geography and French. Months had passed since my encounter on the mountain. I had not climbed in the Reeks since. When I tried to share the images that tormented me, that lived with me as clearly as ever, Callum looked at me with sadness in his eyes. He told me Dylan had mentioned it; and then he changed the subject!

I started to lose track of time, almost every waking minute I was haunted by the sounds of a forgotten evil. Then, one day, both my sons visited me. They had arranged for a doctor to visit. It seemed they had decided I needed to go into hospital. The doctor asked me about my experience on the mountain. I told him the exact truth. The doctor agreed with my sons, and I was taken into hospital.

It's over a year now since I came to this hospital. I hate it. It doesn't help me forget the day I met the… remaining… whatever it was. Ghost… memory… whatever... whatever. It lives on in my head with vivid clarity. The boys rarely come to see me. When they do, I'm afraid to talk of my last visit to the Reeks. It's not surprising they think I've cracked. If I make an effort to talk about it, they invariably clam up. But I have nothing else to say, nothing else to discuss, so when they visit, little is said.

Three or four days ago now, Dylan came to visit. From somewhere, I suddenly found the courage to ask him to bring me a map of the Reeks. To my surprise, he said he had one in the car and he would get it for me. When he brought it, I found the obscure path that had taken me to my chilling encounter and pointed to it.

"Dylan, please, go there. Go alone. Go carefully."

Yesterday, Dylan came to see me again. He didn't say much, but he held my hand.

"Dad, he knew I was your son… the remaining..."

I suddenly noticed there were tears in his eyes.

"Dad, we've got work to do. You're coming home tomorrow."

Team Knibs

Life At Ninety-Nine

Today has been a dead loss for me; I've got nothing done, and now at evening time, I'm so tired.

Another day wasted, and at my time of life I need to make the most of every hour God sends.

After all, having got this far, I fully expect to make it to a hundred. Ninety-nine is no age to clock out of the factory of life. Let's get that century on the board first, and at ninety-nine why should I buzz around anyway? I've earned my rest periods, sure I have. Now where's that other bottle.

The doctor said I should drink at least one bottle of porter each day, and as I had been away for a few days, I had some catching up to do... and I am feeling very tired.

I look out the window, robins picking at the greenfly on my roses; crows feeding on the top tiny branches of the fir-trees dropping the tiny green berries here and there; bees busy at the nasturtium flowers on my window box. I have to do some work. That hedge needs cutting, where are the clippers, it badly needs edging.

Oh, here comes the rain! No need to sharpen the clippers after all. Tomorrow is another day. I'll make up my nightcap prescribed by the doctor. Life is great at ninety-nine. Cheers.

One of the regular exercises at Knibs sessions is to write an opening sentence, then pass it on round the circle for each member present to add a following sentence or two. The above is an example of such an exercise, the contributors on this occasion were Jo, Hazel, Tim, Mick & Kate.

Kate Ahern

Caragh Lake

Caragh Lake, dear Caragh Lake,
You are so still today
Majestic mountains of the Reeks
Shielding you from the wind and rain
Your gentle green and purple hills
Wrapped in heather
Small green fields
With sheep grazing here and there

I see small boats fishing for trout
Enjoying the sun, scenery and serenity
I hear the trickle of water
Cascading down the hillside
Hurrying to reach lake and sea

The scent of damp moss,
The glory of the golden furze
You are so beautiful
You give me peace
You make me dream
But not of riches or worldly things

It's good to be alive and in your company
Yet people pass you by,
They don't seem to see or feel
Your power, your grandeur and tranquility

T William Powell

The Crime Of Letdown And Punishment

He trudged into the pub and slumped himself down at the table; he realised he didn't know which public house he'd just entered, and he hadn't got anything to drink either. "Sheesh and begorra" thought Seamus, went to the bar, got himself something of an alcoholic constitution, and returned to his seat.

What a day, he thought to himself. I hate the ruddy job, it pays me barely enough to come in here and drink enough to forget about the sorry state that I seem to be in, and now it looks like Margot is never coming back. He hadn't noticed someone else had sat down across the table, and almost jumped when he put his hand out to get his glass and looked up and saw this somewhat bulky presence opposite him.

"Jaysus feckin' Christ" he spouted, as he noticed someone else had appeared at his table. The someone else smiled, put his glass back on the table, and then emitted a little chuckle.

"Mistaken identity, buddy. My name's not Jesus." He then supped some more from his glass and Seamus thought he seemed a pleasant enough soul to have joined him as he sat to contemplate the hapless complexity of being Seamus and how the feck would he ever get Margot back.

"No, I didn't think it was," said Seamus. The large form laughed more robustly this time.

"Buddy, I didn't think you *did* think it was. You just seemed a tad, how shall I say, surprised by my being here. Which seemed a strange response in itself, given that you're sat in a bar. Or 'pub' as you call them over here."

Seamus had not got far into his pint, so was able to grasp this looming shape opposite him seemed from his voice to be of a somewhat American origin.

"You're American, are you?" The large bulk laughed once more, and then said,

"Well roast my butt in the caverns of hell, the man's a genius." He laughed some more, then looked a little less jocular as he moved his top half towards the table.

"Yes, Seamus or whatever you're called, I am indeed an American. I spend some time here though, as it happens." Seamus was stunned, again.

He knows my name he thought. He gulped some more alcoholic sustenance and then looked back again, rather less relaxed and louche than his new colleague had looked a few seconds before.

"Er, how do you know my name?" At this the larger human form positively erupted with laughter. After which, he wiped his mouth of its beer and spittle and looked back at Seamus.

"So you are a Seamus?" There was no immediate response from the rather bemused local, so he carried on.

"I just said Seamus or whatever you're called, buddy. It's just the name I tend to call folk I meet over here. Y'know, like you might talk about me as the yank you met in the bar."

Reassured by this apparent evidence that the large presence opposite did not already know him, Seamus spoke up again.

"Oh that's a relief, I thought you'd come to kill me or something when you knew my name. I thought Margot had taken out a contract on me or something." There was a moment's change of facial expression on the large form sat opposite dressed in mingle-in clothes, but Seamus didn't notice it, and the two of them shared a drink or two more and Seamus felt rather cheered by meeting him. It never occurred to him that his new friend hadn't introduced himself yet.

It was getting on for an hour later, with most of the conversational chatter having exited the mouth of Seamus, that he finally asked his new buddy his name.

"Oh my name? You can call me Al." With which he then did an impromptu chord or two of the Paul Simon song, and smiled to himself as he thought *"Of course, I'm in Ireland, the green one probably doesn't remember Paul Simon."*

"I'm going to see him this month," said Seamus.

"Huh?"

"I'm going to see Simon and Garfunkel this month, they're over here you know." Al had been supping as Seamus said that, and he almost choked on it as it transpired his little rural buddy *did* know who Paul Simon was.

"Oh holy shit, yes of course; I'd seen they were playing over here. Sorry man, I thought my little musical link was lost on you there. Muchoas apologios." On asking Seamus where they were playing and being told, when Seamus finally managed to emit words through his laughter, that it was on the bridge over troubled water, much mutual laughter ensued. It was not long after that, whether Seamus realised he didn't know anything about what Al did for a living or not, that it emerged that Al was a business man.

"What business is it?" asked Seamus.

"None of your goddamn business" came the swift, stinging reply, though Al didn't keep the deadpan serious face for more than a moment, and the two were laughing and conversing like old buddies for another few minutes when, just as one little piece of chatter that would drift into the forgotten air no doubt, Seamus happened to mention he wouldn't mind Al helping do a bit of business for him.

"Oh really, what's that then?" So Seamus relayed the tale of how he and some friends had been sorely let down by this worthless piece of apparent human form who'd said he'd help them get some work fashioned into a saleable shape, and how they'd gone on and done it themselves anyway, eventually, and how he wished the sorry piece of shite would die.

"Well man, people die a lot these days. You might say that's not far removed from my line of business. Where is he, this execrable specimen?"

"Kenmare." Al's face lightened as he heard that.

"Not a problem, buddy. I gotta go there anyway." Seamus thought Al was just joshing of course, when he asked how much it would cost and Al said how much have you got, and Seamus could only find a ten euro note in his wallet, and Al said "Not to worry man, I think I know the vat of slime you're talking about; it'll be a pleasure to take him out, just give me the note," they both laughed heartily. Seamus probably didn't even remember that he gave Al the ten euro, and as he made his way home out of the pub he couldn't remember entering, he didn't know that in a week's time he'd be stunned to pick up *The Kerryman* and read of the murder of the very same execrable person he'd talked to Al about. He wasn't to know that Al knew precisely who he'd mentioned, and already had a contract for him in his pocket, for a good deal more than ten euro.

He just thought "A murder here in Kenmare? Stone me, it's not as if we're in Dublin gangland," sighed, and then smiled as he had a vague memory of how he'd joked with that bloke he met in the pub about giving him a note to take the wretched jerkin out.

Imagine that, thought Seamus, that would've been the greatest tenner I ever spent. He smiled, picked up his keys, and went off to another job, or another pub, who knows? And for that matter who knows where Al is now, and whether he's in a pub or doing another job?

Hazel Endean

Shelters

The shop doorway is wide and deep. In wartime, the blackout means total darkness; not a chink of light to be seen anywhere. Only luminous discs, glowing on coat lapels, give an indication of people passing by. In this shelter from wind and rain, I enjoy illicit cuddles with a man whose face smells of 'Ashes of Roses' and resembles Gary Cooper.

The cellar of our home is turned into an air-raid shelter. Whenever the siren sounds, we troop down a flight of cold stone steps, to an even colder room, where we huddle together, listening to the far-off exploding bombs. My father is the local A.R.P. warden; he goes outside, checking for possible incendiaries and making sure that neighbours are safe until the all-clear is given.

On the verandah of the clubhouse, my love and I hold hands, kiss, swear undying love for ever and ever. Starry nights, when our heartbeats are the only sound in the stillness. We are locked into another time, far from families and home. Here, we can make-believe we are the only ones who matter in the whole wide world. First love, young love; a time both dear and precious, in our own special shelter which we never want to leave.

Reluctantly, we head for home, joining the queue in the bus-shelter. Women chattering about husbands, men talking about everything except their wives; back to the humdrum once more. Never mind, tomorrow we can escape to our own special shelter again.

Carol Clifford

Which Piece Is Home

Home is where the heart is
That's what they all say
But if the heart split where it lands
Which piece is home?

The one tied to earth
With its cares and its woes
Or the one soaring free
With its spirit unbarred
To the dreams of a lifetime
Which no place can enclose

Which piece is home?
The safe dull routine
Marching steadily onwards
To deaths dreary theme

Give me unsure, unsafe
High soaring dream
Which lures the soul star-wards
Through a dark empty night

Give me the body, frail as it is
To follow that dream
And to catch the last note
As I fall in mid-flight.

Jo Scanlon

Killorglin Then And Now

I got off the train in Killorglin Railway Station way back in 1946 feeling rather apprehensive, as I was to commence teaching in the Intermediate School the following morning. Having spent my first night in the Railway Hotel, I walked to school to be warmly welcomed by the principal, Mr Jack O'Dwyer who introduced me to the other two members of the staff. Little did I think then that I would spend many, many years in this small country town, as it then was.

World War II had ended the previous year, and most of the traffic consisted of lorries transporting loads of turf to Dublin's Phoenix Park, to be piled up there for distribution until alternative fuel should be more readily available.

The town depended mainly on the agricultural community. The old creamery in Annadale Road was a hive of activity each morning. It was nothing unusual to see a long line of donkeys and carts stretching away back into town and over the bridge. Woe betide the man who dared break the queue. The butter-maker was a lady from Limerick, and the Creamery manager was Michael O'Sullivan, a man who could relate many a tale involving the creamery during his time and back in the time of the 'Troubles'. For example, on the night of the Hillville ambush in 1920, two of the Black and Tans were killed. Reinforcements were sent from Killarney with orders to attack the first large building on the right as they came into town. However, instead of coming directly from Killarney, they mistakenly took the Beaufort road and attacked the old creamery, the first large building on the right on the Annadale Road. Troops ran riot in Killorglin that night causing havoc and terror. The 'new' creamery stands on the Tralee Road now, with no sign of a lady butter-maker or even one donkey and cart.

There was a big monthly cattle fair held on the street; rather daunting to a newcomer. The beautiful song, 'She moved through the fair' took on a different meaning for me, as I proceeded slowly, weaving my way round restless beasts closely guarded by men with stout sticks protruding dangerously from underneath their arms. However, it was good business for the town, as also were the thriving turkey markets before Christmas. The first factory set up here was Wensel Leather, which lost out to foreign competitors, and for a brief period we had a fishing tackle factory in the Fair Field.

In those far-off days, we did have a Railway Station which unfortunately shut down in 1960, a sad day for the town. We also had a hotel, now the Manor Inn. The main source of entertainment was the Oisin Cinema whose proprietor, Patrick 'Duffy' O'Shea was always first in Co. Kerry to show the latest film. Now in this age of affluence, we have lost our train, our hotel and our cinema.

In my first year in the school, better known as 'The Carnegie', we had eighty pupils and four teachers. I spent thirty-seven years there, first under the principalship of Mr Jack O'Dwyer, who showed great interest in his pupils as he guided them through the poor times of the fifties and sixties. No school buses then, no uniforms, no transport except bicycles from all the outlying areas... Castlemaine, Cromane, Glenbeigh and even as far away as Keel. And for warmth, only the old turf fire, later replaced by central heating.

In 1951 Mr O'Dwyer was succeeded by his son Joe, who had started as a pupil in the old Carnegie on the same day as I had come to teach there. Thanks to the then minister Donogh O'Malley's free education, and indeed thanks to Joe's diligence and high sense of discipline, numbers went up by leaps and bounds. Today, the old school has moved to a palatial building with modern spacious classrooms, a huge choice of subjects, an all-weather playing pitch, and with over seven hundred pupils and over forty teachers - a far cry from the original four. I grew very attached to the old Carnegie, having spent so long there. We often lingered for a chat and a smoke in the staff-room after school hours. I am sure that past pupils as well as teachers have happy memories of their days there.

The annual Saint Patrick's Day School Concert was always a sell-out. Preparations went on for some weeks ahead. Classes were somewhat disrupted by rehearsals, and many of the boys were more than willing to lend a hand at setting up props, scenery etc. Mrs Ovens, Killorglin's music teacher, opened the proceedings with a colourful children's operetta, where many of her young pupils, the 'tiny tots' of yesterday, were later to shine in Drama and of course in Pantomime in our indispensable C Y M S hall. One such Tiny Tot was so much at home on the stage that, while the children's chorus rendered with feeling 'The General's Fast Asleep', our little 'General', Declan Mangan, nodded off comfortably in his chair. No stage fright for him then or ever since down through the years, indeed, he has gone on to produce our fiftieth panto.

When the 'Old Carnegie' closed its doors as a school it was certainly not left there to fall into ruin. While retaining its original classic frontage, the remainder has been completely refurbished and enlarged. It is now a state of the art Day-Care Centre, thanks to the local Saint Vincent De Paul society, who deserve the highest commendation for their foresight. Every day senior citizens meet here for a chat, a lunch, a game of cards, or even exercises. They can visit the resident chiropodist and physiotherapist; and it's a godsend for these people to be driven to and from the centre. Otherwise, they would not meet their old friends from one end of the year to the next. As the years moved on, we had our own T.D. Chub O'Connor who worked hard to introduce industry to the town. Klinge Pharmaceuticals was our first major factory followed by Liebig and later by Fujisawa (now part of Astellas), all of which have given enormous employment. Where the Railway Station once stood we now have the internationally known Fexco (Foreign Exchange), founded in 1958 by the courageous entrepreneur Brian MacCarthy, who has really put Killorglin on the map. Indeed, a returned exile would scarcely recognise his native town today, industry having brought about such an increase in population and wealth. All roads leading to the town have now become our modern suburbia. Cafés and restaurants abound. The new town centre is Library Place, an extensive complex including Library, Co. Council Offices, Tourist Office, apartments, retail units and a children's playground. And all this looking out on an elaborate square, complete with fountains, seating and shrubbery, all erected over an ultra modern underground car-park.

Killorglin people are still the same warm friendly folk they were in the forties and, I'm sure, long before that. One thing they have, and will never lose, is Puck Fair: that unique festival presided over by a goat who somehow seems sad on Scattering evening as he leaves us, if we are to believe his song.

"My heart fills with sadness this Scattering evening.
I'm leaving you all to go back to the Reeks.
The buskers, the dancers, the gigs and magicians,
The bands, Birds' Bazaar and the stalls in the street.
So, strike up your music once more just to cheer me
Let the echoes resound o'er the Laune loud and clear
Three cheers for Killorglin and all her good people
Is go mbeirimid beo ar an am so airis."

Is go mbeirimid beo ar an am so airis -
                That we may all be alive and happy this time twelve months

Notes on contributors:

Kate Ahern was born in Milltown, County Kerry. The youngest of nine children, she went to the Presentation Convent, Milltown. She has lived in Killorglin for forty-eight years. A contributor to 'Breacadh' and 'Ripples From The Laune'.

Carol Clifford (1944-2006) was born in Omagh County Tyrone. Lived in England and then Kildare before settling in Castlemaine in the mid 90s. Her own description of herself reads, "...had incarnations, as a nurse, an academic and now poet, which manages to combine the experiences of all three". A contributor to 'Breacadh' and 'Ripples From The Laune'.

Mary Collins was born in Millstreet County Cork. A retired doctor, she now lives in Glenbeigh. She has had work published in 'Irelands Own', 'Breacadh' and 'Ripples From The Laune'.

Hazel Endean was born in Lancashire, England and later moved to Cornwall. In 1973 she came to Dooks, Co. Kerry. Her first love is writing; other interests are watercolour painting, playing keyboard, table tennis and short mat bowls. An avid reader, she is also a scrabble and crossword fanatic. Hazel has had articles published in Ireland's Own, and on R.T.E.

Jack O'Dwyer was born in Killorglin, County Kerry. He moved to London to work in the banking industry, but returned to his home town on retirement. A contributor to 'Breacadh' and 'Ripples From The Laune'.

Mary Foley-Taylor is a native of Killorglin who returned after twenty years in New York. Discovery of an old family grave in 1972 led her on decades of research on local families and their extended branches. She studied Accountancy in Poughkeepsie, N.Y. and History at UCC and Queen's University, Belfast.

Mick Jones moved from Evesham, Worcestershire (UK) to Glounaguillagh, three miles outside Killorglin in October 2004. Originally an orchestral viola player with the BBC, he then nailed a job as 'the mad fiddle player' for a busy Birmingham rock band; spent nearly five years in the insurance industry; and then fifteen (and counting) in music education. Currently striving to find more time for writing prose, poetry and music.

T William Powell (1958-), born in the eastern English village hamlet of Barton Mills, first emigrated minor scale down to Kent, where he worked as a vegan chef and whole-foods shuffler; before emigrating larger scale across the water to Co. Kerry, from where he's been writing prose, poetry and freelance journalism ever since. The published pieces are few, but hey, here's a few more...   timwpowell@eircom.net

Jo Scanlon was born in Ballyduff, County Waterford, and has lived in Killorglin since 1946. A retired teacher, she now enjoys reading, writing and working at her computer. She has written scripts for local stage performances and contributed to 'Ripples From The Laune'.